The Ultimate Simulation

Does believing something make it real, true or both?

If it were true, crazy people could fly.

Tom Long

The Ultimate Simulation

Copyright © 2019, 2022 by Thomas R. Long

ALL RIGHTS RESERVED

Unless otherwise noted, all Scripture references are from the

The New King James Version. (1982). Nashville: Thomas Nelson. Used by permission.

Published by

Tom Long Books

18896 Greenwell Springs Road

Greenwell Springs, LA 70739

ISBN 978-0-9718631-2-5

Printed in the U.S., the U.K. and Australia

For Worldwide Distribution

Dedication

To my late wife who loved, encouraged, prayed for and put up with me. Her continued pointing to "What is the Lord saying?" kept me going when I didn't want to.

I also wanted to thank my friend Nickolas G. for his constructive criticism.

Contents

Introduction	9
Chapter 1 A Pre-Simulation	47
Chapter 2 The Simulation	63
Chapter 3 The Purpose of the Simulation	65
Chapter 4 The Nature of God	73
Chapter 5 One-Trick Ponies	79
Chapter 6 The Soul	85
Chapter 7 Players	109
Chapter 8 The Multiverse	117
Chapter 9 Dimensions and Portals	121
Chapter 10 A Primary Field	123
Chapter 11 Entanglement	129
Chapter 12 A Hologram	131
Chapter 13 Black Holes	133
Chapter 14 Forces and Particles	141
Chapter 15 Eternal Life and God's Love	145
Chapter 16 Were We Seeded?	147
Chapter 17 What's Next?	151
Conclusions	155

Preface

This book is about changing your perspective. Before you jump to the sections about the simulation, read the Introduction. In order to understand someone's conclusions, you should understand their perspective. The Introduction is not complete, but is used to highlight revelations. I changed names just because.

A few years ago considering a simulation on the scale of our universe was unthinkable. Because of the strides in hardware, software and Moore's Law, we can conceive in the near future it should be possible. Has some intelligence, real or artificial, already done it and if so, are we in it?

This book explores some of the possibilities if we are living in a simulation. Specifically, how we view God and His Word.

I don't claim to have all the answers. I am putting forth possibilities.

This book is meant to be a work-in-progress and it is my intent to reprint when more possibilities are explored.

Religion is filled with absolutes, life should be filled with possibilities.

Introduction

K-leb was born in the Bronx, New York during the 2nd Great War. His father had insisted on the name, being both a chaplain and a comic book fan. This is his story.

My first recollection is living in a second floor apartment in a city. We had a refrigerator where ice was put in the top compartment which kept things cool below. Once a day the ice man would come by in a wagon with sawdust covered ice. My mom would buy a block of ice and the man would carry it upstairs with a big set off tongs. Most times he would offer me a sliver of ice as a treat.

I was the number two son. Clark was my older brother, Lex and Perry where my younger brothers. We were all separated by about three years. Mom had always wanted a daughter, but it was not to be.

I remember being shipped off to my grandparents when Perry was born. I went to kindergarten there for about six months. By this time, my dad had returned from the war and started a church in Baltimore, Md.

Nothing unusual about my childhood as I recall, other than the mischief four boys can get into. Every night after dinner, my dad would read Bible stories and we all had our assigned tasks. With the age difference, we boys didn't really hang out together. We were pretty much on our own.

The Ultimate Simulation

Things started to change when I was 12. The light on my bicycle was out, so at dusk I decided to ride my brother's bike to a store two blocks away to get a bulb. There was a hill outside our house and at the bottom was a traffic light. I was coming down the hill when a '47 Chevy coupe didn't see me and turned in front of me. I hit him head-on. My forehead took out his windshield on the passenger side, my arm hit the 'A' pillar before I rolled off his hood onto the pavement. The driver did stop. I ended up with a broken arm and a spot on my forehead about the size of a quarter they put a patch over.

Afterwards, I started to get serious about God. I remember giving my heart to the Lord around 12. I've always known I was a teacher.

A lot of the Bible stories didn't make sense to me. It was at that time I started praying for understanding. I talked to God, but I never heard Him or if I did, I didn't recognize who was talking. I would ask questions of my parents and others, but for the most part, all I ever got were clichés. "It's not for us to know", "God works in mysterious ways", "When we get to heaven..." or "You're just a child, someday..." None of these were acceptable. The way I read the Bible, either all of it was true or none of it was. I decided that if it was true, then it should be demonstrable.

In my midteens, I started looking at all religions and disciplines to see what would work. The only thing I found could backup their claims was Yoga. I learned over months, if I meditated certain ways, I could control my

The Ultimate Simulation

heart rate or make pain disappear. I checked out all the 'New Age' claims. It looked like I was making progress as I experimented with all kinds of things except drugs. Each time before I tried something, I would ask the Lord for protection, understanding and to close the door if it was not right. I developed a sense where I could tell if someone was thinking about me and if I would meditate, I could see images of that person.

I believe we all build a model of how the universe works, based upon our talents, education and experience. Some people are more inquisitive than others. Each time I found something that worked, I adjusted the model. I was still praying daily for understanding. By the time I reached twenty, I wasn't adjusting my model by large amounts, just smaller tweaks.

Eastern meditation is about emptying yourself. It occurred to me that if you are empty, you can't protect yourself from being possessed or oppressed.

Luke 11:24-26 [24] "When an unclean spirit goes out of a man, he goes through dry places, seeking rest; and finding none, he says, 'I will return to my house from which I came.' [25] And when he comes, he finds *it* swept and put in order. [26] Then he goes and takes with *him* seven other spirits more wicked than himself, and they enter and dwell there; and the last *state* of that man is worse than the first."

This was one of my first revelations. I was praying about meditation when I saw a glass half-full of caked mud. No matter what the glass did, it couldn't get rid of the dried mud. However, if the glass positioned itself in a flow of water, the water would loosen the mud and float it up and out of the glass.

> **Revelation: Christian meditation is not about emptying; it's about filling with the water of the Holy Spirit and the Word.**

Ephesians 5:22-27 [22] Wives, submit to your own husbands, as to the Lord. [23] For the husband is head of the wife, as also Christ is head of the church; and He is the Savior of the body. [24] Therefore, just as the church is subject to Christ, so *let* the wives *be* to their own husbands in everything.

[25] Husbands, love your wives, just as Christ also loved the church and gave Himself for her, [26] <u>that He might sanctify and cleanse her with the washing of water by the word</u>, [27] that He might present her to Himself a glorious church, not having spot or wrinkle or any such thing, but that she should be holy and without blemish.

I had come to the conclusion that Christianity was the only religion not based on works, special knowledge, or mental capacity, but faith. It finally made sense, faith was the great equalizer. If God was not a respecter of persons, then this appeared to answer one of my questions. I made a commitment to pursue God at all costs.

Eventually, I crossed some boundary in my experimenting and was contacted by an angel, telling me to stop or else.

The Ultimate Simulation

I was crushed and felt I had been setup to fail. Which in hindsight, I was. I blamed God for the setup, because I had asked Him to protect and guide me. I didn't realize that ignorance of the law is no excuse.

I shut down my experimenting and took a break. I needed time to deal with my resentment. I had been praying for understanding for twelve years and while the things I found out were amazing, I couldn't talk to most people about them. Also, I was coming to realize that with understanding comes responsibility and I found I couldn't handle it. So I quit praying, but still believed.

To go back, my father was a good man, but a perfectionist and very prideful. He was well educated, knew six languages and prided himself on doing the New York Times Sunday crossword in ink. My mom was also well educated and enjoyed crossword puzzles. He would try to fix everything, in which he was mostly successful. All of us boys have had to deal with pride. But without a sister we were love and relationship challenged. I also have a great love of puzzles.

At eighteen I enlisted, before being drafted, and signed up for the longest school I could get. This worked out to eighteen months of electronics training in analog and digital computers. The transistor was in its infancy and small scale integrated circuits had just been invented.

One Sunday, while in training, I went to the base chapel. The sermon was so bad; it was all I could do not to leave. This wasn't Christianity, it was communism. As I

The Ultimate Simulation

was walking back to the barracks, I was complaining to the Lord about the sermon and the chaplain when I heard, "**Are you responsible for what you hear or what He says**"?

That day I learned I could get revelation from a turnip, if I open my eyes and ears to the Lord and don't judge. It's hard not to judge what the other person is saying, but we need to listen beyond for what the Holy Spirit is saying. Judgment shuts down communication. It was the beginning of the Lord talking to me in questions.

After serving my time in the military I went to work for NASA as a contractor on the consoles for the Apollo missions. After the contract, I went to work for a process control manufacturer as a field repair technician. It was there that I met my wife, Lois. She was the first person I found who loved the Lord more than I. In addition, we could talk about almost everything. On our third date, I proposed as I had all but given up on finding anyone I could talk to. My ideas about love were on both ends of the spectrum. I had come to the conclusion that you couldn't love anyone until you could love everyone. But practically, I was a novice. While we were sitting on her couch after proposing, I felt a presence in the room. I closed my eyes and immediately saw a picture of a balding middle aged man smiling. I had never seen her father or met any of her family. On my first trip to her home, atop her mother's piano, I saw a picture of the man I had seen. It was her father, who had died twelve years prior.

The Ultimate Simulation

Eventually, we got married and bought a town home. The company I was with was transitioning from discrete hardware to computer control. I decided I wanted to be the first person to know both. I started night school for programming. My wife was also doing night school in business. We only saw each other on weekends.

Things were quiet. We weren't going to church although we attended a Bible study. We read some Edgar Cayce books and joined a group. While it was interesting, it wasn't going anywhere. There was so much error we dropped out.

We moved to five acres in the country and enjoyed gardening. It relieved a lot of the work stress. We started attending a Methodist church in a village about ten miles away.

I received the Holy Spirit watching Oral Roberts on TV.

One Sunday, we were late for church. I was speeding on a back country road when I heard, **"Is there such a thing as speeding for Jesus"?**

Of course I knew the answer. How can He who is all authority condone rebellion against authority? So I slowed down. Speeding and lack of mercy for challenged drivers is an ongoing issue.

We were active in the church and I decided to go to Methodist seminary. I lasted two semesters before I

The Ultimate Simulation

couldn't resolve situational ethics and other issues I felt disagreed with scripture.

One day while driving to seminary, I was tired of carrying the resentment towards God. It had been almost ten years since I quit praying. I repented and felt a tangible weight lift off my shoulders. Then I felt stupid for carrying this around for so long. I heard God again. **"Welcome back."** Now I really felt stupid.

Another day while driving, I heard. **"You amaze me".** I knew this was not a good thing and waited for the other shoe to drop. **"I'm amazed at how much your model of the universe is correct. There's just one thing".** Now I knew I was in trouble. **"I didn't teach it to you. I want you to forget all that you think you know about the universe and me and let's start over".**

How do you do that? Most of us incorporate what we believe into our identity. How do you reset your identity?

I took a break from thinking about it for almost fifteen years. I was successful at the process control company. Computer control was just getting started so I decided to go to night school to learn programming. I wanted to be the first person in the company to know both hardware and software. Eventually I transitioned from hardware to programming. Computer control was in its infancy and these computers had 16K memory with no disk. Everything was loaded with paper tape through a

The Ultimate Simulation

Teletype machine in machine language. There were not a lot of programmers who could do this type of work. Our operating system ran in 2k of memory. Most programmers were high caliber, but every now and then we got a dud.

Once, I had been working on a programming problem for two days. I finally prayed and asked the Lord for help. I was stuck. Ten minutes later, the dud came into my office and said something stupid. A correlation went off in my head and the solution was right there. "Oh Lord, how could you do this to me? Using the dud to give me the answer. I have ridiculed him so many times. Forgive me."

I moved from programming to management and was fairly successful after having to deal with the switch from self satisfaction to deriving satisfaction from my employees doing a good job. I could see the need for a new position, so I spent a year and made myself the most qualified before floating the idea. I got the management job. However, I was put under a micro-manager who wouldn't give me the authority to do my job. After six months it was time to exit.

We started our own business. Still went to church, not so much for instruction but for fellowship. We struggled for three years to get things profitable until an employee theft put us into bankruptcy. We lost everything, our house and savings. In addition, the IRS gave us a bill for an additional $20,000+. That was a lot of money in 1983.

The Ultimate Simulation

We had read a book by Kenneth Hagan and wanted to go to a church where things were happening in the Spirit. The book talked about Texas. I contacted a friend who had moved to Texas and I got a job. We only had twenty dollars the day of our move and no credit cards. It was 1250 miles and all we could take was in our Datsun wagon and a 4x5 trailer. That day when we said goodbye to our neighbor, he gave me $100.00 which gave us enough to buy gas. "Praise the Lord".

We stayed with our friend until payday, and then found a townhome rental. We didn't have any furniture. The town home we found had a breakfast nook with padded benches. This gave us a place to sleep. Our friend bought us a refrigerator and a mattress. We paid him back over six months. Things were really tight. Over the course of the next year, we visited secondhand stores and found a couch and a couple of chairs. We painted my old Army trunk blue for a coffee table. We didn't have much, but were happy.

After paying monthly business debt, IRS, rent and utilities; we had about $200 dollars for food, clothing and auto expenses. Five months later they took our car, saying there was too much equity in it. The company I was working for loaned me money to buy a used car. It was the favor of God.

We started our search for a church where the Spirit was moving. We finally found a small independent church and settled in. I volunteered to usher. My wife volunteered to help with the children, but was asked to leave (wrong

The Ultimate Simulation

race). Two months later she was in charge of children's church. It's amazing how God works.

It was at this time as we were learning about the manifestations of the Holy Spirit, two things happened. The first was when the pastor offered a challenge to pray with him an hour a day, Monday – Friday, at 5:00A.M. This was in response to Larry Lea's book "Could You Not Tarry For One Hour?" He said if we did this for a month, it would change our lives. I took him up on it. I can testify that it did.

The second thing was we became convicted about not tithing. We barely had enough money for food, but decided to put God to the test. I know we went without for a while, but the time went quickly. In two and a half years we were out of debt. While we were going through it, it seemed impossible and I never would have believed it could be resolved in that amount of time, but it was. No miraculous donations, just faithfulness, prayer and tears. Twice my wife went to the IRS to contest their mismanagement and twice she won.

Malachi 3:10-11 [10] Bring the full tithe into the storehouse, that there may be food in my house. And thereby put me to the test, says the LORD of hosts, if I will not open the windows of heaven for you and pour down for you a blessing until there is no more need. [11] I will rebuke the devourer for you, so that it will not destroy the fruits of your soil, and your vine in the field shall not fail to bear, says the LORD of hosts.[1]

Once you've gone through losing everything, you no longer fear losing anything. I'd rather not, but with God's help I know we'll survive.

> **Revelation: Poverty isn't about money, it's about a lack of faith in the provision of the Lord and the talents He has given you, laziness and blame.**

We have been without and in dire straits several times, but have never been poor.

During this time I was learning to respond to the Holy Spirit. When I first started praying, at most it would take two minutes until I was through my list. In order to fill up the hour, I followed the pastor's lead and prayed in tongues. I usually checked my watch every few minutes to see if time was up. By the end of the first month, I almost always went over.

Praying in tongues caused me to sense a presence.

John 5:19 [19] Then Jesus answered and said to them, "Most assuredly, I say to you, the Son can do nothing of Himself, but what He sees the Father do; for whatever He does, the Son also does in like manner.

---

[1]*The Holy Bible: English Standard Version.* (2016). (Mal 3:10–11). Wheaton, IL: Crossway Bibles.

The Ultimate Simulation

I decided if this was true for Jesus, it should be true for me. Before I'd make a decision, I'd pray. And if I felt the presence of the Holy Spirit, I took it as confirmation.

I did this for several years and things seemed to work out.

I had wanted to get a little pocket recorder and since money was tight, I prayed and felt I got the go ahead. One day as I was driving down the freeway to look for a recorder another question came. **"Will your flesh ever tell you no?"**

> **Revelation: Sensing the presence of the Holy Spirit in response to a Yes/No question usually means "NO!"**

"Father, forgive me for getting this backward, but why didn't you tell me sooner?" **"Because this is the only way you'd learn".**

Ouch! He knows me pretty well.

I went to a Service Merchandise store to look for a recorder. They had the one I wanted for $99, but I had some questions. The clerk behind the counter was engaged in a conversation about fishing and completely ignored me. After five minutes, I gave up. At Service Merchandise you filled out an order slip, paid for your order, and then your order would come down a conveyor belt. I filled out a slip and got in line. There was only one

The Ultimate Simulation

register open and six people ahead of me. After ten minutes, I was next when I felt the presence of the Holy Spirit. What's going on? Lord, you said I could get it. I've waited and I'm next. I decided to put my new revelation to the test. I tore up the slip and left. Albeit grumbling. Before I could get back on the freeway, I felt led to go to an Office Max across the street. Miracle. There was the same recorder for $84. On top of that, it was their last one and a demo for $65. The Lord wasn't telling me He changed His mind about me getting one. He was telling me, **"Not here".**

How I jump to conclusions when told no. Forgive me.

Revelation: When we think we hear from the Lord, there are only four possibilities.

I think I heard from the Lord. It was the Lord and **I responded.**	I think I heard from the Lord. It was the Lord and **I did nothing**.
I think I heard from the Lord. It was not the Lord and **I responded.**	I think I heard from the Lord. It was not the Lord and **I did nothing**.

The Lord blesses me when I respond. Even if I get it wrong, grace mitigates the outcome to my benefit.

Suddenly Revelation 3:15-16 made sense.

The Ultimate Simulation

Revelation 3:15-16 [15] "I know your works, that you are neither cold nor hot. I could wish you were cold or hot. [16] So then, <u>because you are lukewarm, and neither cold nor hot, I will vomit you out of My mouth.</u>

If the Lord tells me to turn right and I turn left; grace applies because I acted in faith. Grace only applies when by faith I respond to Him. There is no grace for he who does nothing.

Ephesians 2:8-9 [8] <u>For by grace you have been saved through faith, and that not of yourselves;</u> *it is* <u>the gift of God,</u> [9] not of works, lest anyone should boast.

> **Revelation: We get to grace through faith. Grace and mercy aren't for when I get it right.**

While the max blessing applies if we get it right, God mitigates the consequences if we get it wrong. It's a win-win. Either way we are still blessed if we respond in faith.

Romans 8:28 [28] <u>And we know that for those who love God all things work together for good, for those who are called according to his purpose.</u>

We know that if we love God, we trust and obey. (Respond)

John 14:15 [15] "<u>If you love me, you will keep my commandments.</u>

The Ultimate Simulation

It was around this time, we were introduced to the ministry of Charles and Francis Hunter. We read the books on "How To Heal The Sick" and watched the video training. We also attended several of their healing explosions. At church, a prayer partner came down with cancer. We prayed and laid hands on him. I was confident he would be healed, but he died. I complained to the Lord and asked why our prayers didn't work. Back came the statement **"I don't trust the keys to a Ferrari to a five year old"**.

It was like an arrow pierced my heart. I was just starting to learn the cost associated with moving deeper in Christ.

> **Revelation: Every ounce of the Spirit requires a pound of flesh.**

We didn't quit, but continued praying for people. I remember the first time a person's headache left in response to prayer.

Hallelujah, it works. Our faith was getting stronger. We graduated from headaches to back pain. I remember the first time cancer was healed. My wife was praying over the phone for a woman just diagnosed with facial skin cancer. The woman claimed her face was heating up. Then the cancer simply fell off. Praise the Lord. Currently, not everyone is healed, but I know the day is coming when they will be.

The Ultimate Simulation

I get upset when people are told you weren't healed because you didn't have enough faith. What about the faith of the person praying? When Jesus raised Lazarus from the dead, Lazarus didn't have any faith. He was dead. I will agree it is always somebody's faith.

Somewhere along the line, I came to the conclusion I was missing the compassion gene. In watching my wife interact with people I saw everything I'm not. I'd be more prone to call down fire than love.

One day she had an 'aha' moment. "What if nobody could go to heaven unless we all went? How would that change the way we act?" Truth is, I was more concerned about myself than others. She started to teach me about becoming "one flesh". We were a team. It took a while for me to be just as excited for her revelations and successes as I was about my own. Being a team is not the same as co-dependency. In a sense, this was the beginning of our kingdom mentality. We are only dependent upon the King. No one person or group of people has it all. She has taught me to recognize the potential in others, when before I was more concerned about the facts of the present and how they affected me. My wife and I both have issues, but we choose to believe we are perfect for each other. The Holy Spirit compels us to choose mercy and grace over our weaknesses.

> **Revelation: Extending mercy and grace rekindles desire.**

The Ultimate Simulation

Working with computers, things are either on or off, black or white or 1 or zero. There is no grey or is it gray? However, there can be an undetermined state (null) or in the case of quantum computers multiple states existing at the same time.

> **Revelation: We are all born in an undetermined state with God.**

This leads to other questions.

Genesis 15:16 ¹⁶ And they shall come back here in the fourth generation, <u>for the iniquity of the Amorites is not yet complete</u>.

This seems to imply that there is a tipping point beyond which we can't fulfill any of the possibilities God has for us or in computer terms we move from undetermined to zero.

1 Samuel 15:3 ³ Now go and strike Amalek and devote to destruction all that they have. Do not spare them, <u>but kill both man and woman, child and infant, ox and sheep, camel and donkey</u>.

How can God love everybody and yet kill Amalek and his people including babies?

I was led to John 3:16.

The Ultimate Simulation

John 3:16 [16] "For God so loved the world, that he gave his only Son, that whoever believes in him should not perish but have eternal life".

Then the question came, "***What isn't said?***"

It doesn't say God so loved people.

> **Revelation, God doesn't love people and where they are, He loves what His word says they can become. It's all about His Will.**

John 1:12 [12] But to all who did receive him, who believed in his name, he gave the right to become children of God,

> **Revelation: The Bible isn't about humanity, it's about the making of the sons of God.**

The Bible is filled with stories of people destroyed. (The flood, Sodom and Gomorrah, Korah in the desert and Amalek among others). When human kind no longer possesses the ability to fulfill His plan and they interfere with it, they become expendable in favor of those that still have possibilities.

God is love, but His love is completely tied to His Will and His Word. His love is always about the fulfillment of His Will. To the extent we pursue His Will through His Word; we can appropriate His love. It is available to all. Unfortunately not all pursue it.

The Ultimate Simulation

John 14:6 ⁶ Jesus said to him, "I am the way, and the truth, and the life. <u>No one comes to the Father except through me.</u>

2 Peter 3:9 ⁹ The Lord is not slow to fulfill his promise as some count slowness, but is patient toward you, <u>not wishing that any should perish, but that all should reach repentance.</u>

Free will then isn't about what we think as daily choices, but the ability to go a way different than the way of flesh or running the program. Animals don't have free will. What is it that gives us this option?

In one of the places we lived, my wife was asked to join a Christian women's group. She went because she wanted to meet other Christian women. After attending several meetings, she said something wasn't right. The group would invite unsuspecting women to a fashion show, then spring the gospel on them. We prayed and were led to a scripture.

Jeremiah 48:10 ¹⁰ <u>Cursed *is* he who does the work of the L</u>ORD <u>deceitfully,</u> And cursed *is* he who keeps back his sword from blood.

While we don't go around with swords stabbing people, we do need to tell them.

She told them and said she couldn't be part of it. They replied with the standard rebellious answer, "If just one person gets saved, it's worth it".

The Ultimate Simulation

The Lord spoke to me concerning this saying **"When people say this. This is what I hear. 'Lord, I don't want to do what you are telling me or spend the time to hear you. I will do what I want or copy what's working down the street and if just one person gets saved. It will be worth it.'"**

Have mercy on us Lord and forgive us. I have done the same thing many times.

> **Revelation: Rebellion cloaked in apparent good is still rebellion. So is copying someone else to make up for a lack of relationship; no matter the outcome.**

At one of the churches we attended, we were in charge of prayer. In addition to leading prayer meetings, we would intercede for church services. I found that if I prayed in tongues for two to three hours, I would start to see things. I began to recognize that I was seeing what would happen in the church service. This allowed us to intercede for these situations. The more I prayed, the less time it took to see. Over time, this reduced to an hour, to a half hour, to fifteen minutes and finally to as soon as I started to pray in tongues.

One night I couldn't sleep and got up. Went into the living room and started to pray. The next morning my wife told me she was awakened in the middle of the night and the room was filled with light. There was a flaming sword on the wall of our bedroom. It stayed there for a long time before disappearing. I was unaware this was

The Ultimate Simulation

going on. She told me about it in the morning. We prayed about what to do with this. After about a week, a prayer partner mentioned a scripture and we knew what we had to do.

Ezekial 33:2-6 [2] "Son of man, speak to your people and say to them, If I bring the sword upon a land, and the people of the land take a man from among them, and make him their watchman, [3] and if he sees the sword coming upon the land and blows the trumpet and warns the people, [4] then if anyone who hears the sound of the trumpet does not take warning, and the sword comes and takes him away, his blood shall be upon his own head. [5] He heard the sound of the trumpet and did not take warning; his blood shall be upon himself. But if he had taken warning, he would have saved his life. [6] But if the watchman sees the sword coming and does not blow the trumpet, so that the people are not warned, and the sword comes and takes any one of them, that person is taken away in his iniquity, but his blood I will require at the watchman's hand.

We took the vision and word to the pastor and elders and were shown the door.

> **Revelation: Real friends are only revealed during duress. You can have all the plastic friends you want if you buy the beer.**

We were led to a friend's church whose main ministry was deliverance. We went through all his training. We had been though deliverance twice and were put in

The Ultimate Simulation

charge of praise and worship. We had met Frank and Ida Mae Hammond, author of Pigs In The Parlor, and Frank Marzullo, both pioneers of the deliverance movement.

On one occasion, Frank Marzullo insisted we be ordained. Frank said he would do it if our pastor didn't want to. Our pastor said he would and did. After several years, the Lord told us to start a church. We prayed about this for a few weeks as I did not want to. I knew what would happen, but being under authority, we went and told the pastor what we were told. It was like we shot him with a betrayal knife and shown the door. Since that time we have reconciled. Lord, when does it get easier?

We started a church in our home. Pioneering a church is one of the hardest things we've ever attempted.

My wife was drawn to the prophetic. We had seen several prophets minister and she wanted more. I was good with it, but I was more a teacher-intercessor. We signed up for the prophetic school from Christian International and went through the first week of training. This was great. It helped me to discern more about what I was hearing and seeing. Since then we completed another week of training.

I was drawn to Acts 14:9.

Acts 14:8-10 [8] Now at Lystra there was a man sitting who could not use his feet. He was crippled from birth and had never walked. [9] He listened to Paul speaking. And Paul, looking intently at him and <u>seeing that he had faith to be</u>

The Ultimate Simulation

made well, [10] said in a loud voice, "Stand upright on your feet." And he sprang up and began walking.

What did Paul see? Can faith be spiritually seen? Is there a physical component of faith?

You guessed it, we prayed. I remembered those strange pictures where you had to defocus your eyes before the picture would emerge. When I prayed for people, I started looking beyond them to see what showed up in my peripheral vision. I don't remember when I started, but I started asking the Holy Spirit to light up the person. At first, I imagined the person as a stick figure and prayed for the part that didn't light up. The more I did this, the more details appeared until I was seeing the whole person. As I developed this, people started seeing results and wondering how I knew about old injuries and stuff. I started seeing oppression and fiery darts of spiritual attacks. The more I practiced the more detail I could see. All I can say concerning spiritual gifts is practice, practice, practice.

Somewhere along the line I developed a series of tools to help understand.

1. Tom's Inverse Rule: "If a thing is true, its inverse is also true".

2. Tom's Missing Rule: "What's missing or what isn't said?"

The Ultimate Simulation

3. Tom's Context Rule: "What is the spirit of the surrounding verses and is there a theme to the chapter?"

Instead of asking the Holy Spirit to light everything that wasn't a problem, could I ask for the Holy Spirit to light up anointing? It has taken a while to correlate what it means when different parts light up. However, I still have to ask the Holy Spirit what it means. Never assume. I've made many mistakes leaning on my own understanding. I see new things all the time.

Revelation: When you think you've seen it all or know it all, you're deceived and unteachable. Same applies if you think you know what a scripture means.
There appears to be no end to levels of understanding.
My current understanding is yesterday's news.

Revelation:
Every day there is new manna available.
No matter how well you know something, open your ears, eyes and heart and read it again.
Believing you will receive over time turns into knowing you will receive.

The Ultimate Simulation

Romans 8:26 ²⁶ Likewise the Spirit helps us in our weakness. <u>For we do not know what to pray for as we ought, but the Spirit himself intercedes for us with groanings too deep for words.</u>

As I grew deeper in prayer, the Lord said **"Never pray against anything or anyone. It's a curse."**

James 3:10 ¹⁰ <u>Out of the same mouth proceed blessing and cursing</u>. My brethren, these things ought not to be so.

I had to change all my binding and other negative prayers. I had always wondered if I bind the devil, how does he get free? Truth is I don't have authority over the devil, just his power. Binding the devil is one of those things that makes your flesh feel like you're accomplishing something, but does absolutely nothing in the spiritual realm except sow doubt and unbelief.

Luke 10:19 ¹⁹ Behold<u>, I give you the authority to trample on serpents and scorpions, and over all the power of the enemy,</u> and nothing shall by any means hurt you.

Snakes and scorpions are creatures of the dust. In reality, dust is what we have dominion over.

> **Revelation: I have authority over the devils power to interfere with my God given dominion.**

In dealing with troubleshooting technical issues, most people can't communicate objectively. They tell you

The Ultimate Simulation

their frustrations or emotions, but almost never the facts about the problem. In dealing with people over the phone, I developed what I call the "See Spot Run" approach. Are they in the right building? Are they in front of the equipment? Do they know what the equipment looks like? Is it plugged in? Is it turned on? You get the idea. Most of the time I think God takes that approach with us. Most people in prayer lines are the same way. They will tell you symptoms and seldom want to deal with the underlying issues. "God heal me without pain and don't ask me to change, because I like the way I am." That is the way of flesh, not the way of faith.

> **Revelation: The Lord takes us the easiest way we'll go.**

Some require only a whisper, while people like me often need a two by four.

> **Revelation: Until a person is willing to accept the truth about their situation, healing or deliverance is probably not in the cards.**

     I decided I was like an ant trying to communicate with the Lord of all. I didn't know how to pray because I didn't know what the issues and questions were. Let alone the language issue.

The Ultimate Simulation

Corinthians 14:2 ² For one who speaks in a tongue speaks not to men but to God; for no one understands him, but he utters mysteries in the Spirit.

I thought if my spirit knows, then if I could interpret my tongue I would gain insight. I started practicing it. "Soul, what is the issue I most need to deal with"? Then I would pray a short reply in tongues. Afterward asking the Holy Spirit to interpret what I just prayed. It took a while, but I started being able to interpret my own tongue. My effectiveness in prayer increased dramatically when I learned my own issues. If you have trouble facing the truth, don't do this. Sometimes it's brutal.

Hebrews 12:6 ⁶ For whom the LORD loves He chastens, And scourges every son whom He receives.

This led to a problem. Many Spirit filled churches have the same person give a tongue and then someone gives what they believe is an interpretation. How come the interpretation is always a reply from God? If according to the above scripture, tongues are talking to God, how come all we ever get is the response? "The Lord says…", "My little children…" etc. I started asking for the interpretation of the tongue. My, my, my, what things were revealed. I decided to let sleeping dogs lie. I've seen enough doors.

One point of clarity. I'm not saying that the supposed interpretation is not from God. I'm saying it's not an interpretation of the tongue. I'm also tired of hearing about warring tongues or that Satan can't understand

The Ultimate Simulation

tongues. I don't know of any scripture backing up either of those claims.

1 Corinthians 13:1 ¹ Though I speak with <u>the tongues of men and of angels</u>, and have not charity, I am become as sounding brass, or a tinkling cymbal.

There appears to be only two tongues, men and angels. Since Satan is a fallen angel, he would understand angelic tongues. Since he also tempts man, he would also understand mankind's tongues.

Once during a deliverance session, I heard the Holy Spirit say, ***"Don't deliver a person from something until they are ready to be delivered to the Lord."***

Luke 11:24-26 ²⁴ <u>When the unclean spirit is gone out of a man</u>, he walketh through dry places, seeking rest; and finding none, he saith, I will return unto my house whence I came out. ²⁵ And when he cometh, he findeth it swept and garnished. ²⁶ Then goeth he, and taketh to him seven other spirits more wicked than himself; and they enter in, and dwell there: <u>and the last state of that man is worse than the first.</u>

> **Revelation: The Lord will not heal you against your will and you cannot be delivered from your friends.**

Mark 6:4-6 ⁴ But Jesus said to them, "<u>A prophet is not without honor except in his own country, among his own relatives, and in his own house.</u>" ⁵ <u>Now He could do no mighty work there, except that He laid His hands on a few sick people and healed</u> *them*. ⁶ And He marveled because of

The Ultimate Simulation

their unbelief. Then He went about the villages in a circuit, teaching.

Is it just me or am I reading the scripture wrong? Is the great commission about planting churches or making disciples of Christ? Being a preacher's kid, I am all too familiar with metrics and goals in the church. In fact, it jaded me for a long time. My main goal was to ride my motorcycle into the church and tell people to get a life. I saw the majority of the church as existing for a heavenly mansion in the sweet bye and bye, but almost no one living for Him. One of the biggest thorns in my side was the doctrine of eternal security. Just say this prayer, it's eternally decided and you will know beyond a shadow of a doubt that you are saved. Hogwash!

While there are some occasions when He works unilaterally, everything I see about my future is "Quid Pro Quo".

Matthew 5:7 ⁷Blessed *are* the merciful, for they shall obtain mercy.

Matthew 6:33 ³³But seek first the kingdom of God and his righteousness, and all these things will be added to you.

There are hundreds of scripture about us pursuing Him and the rewards. There are also hundreds of scriptures about what happens if we do not. If God saves us regardless of what we believe and do, then free will is a joke and the scripture is in error.

The Ultimate Simulation

> **Revelation – Salvation isn't a destination, it is what occurs because we choose to become like Him and act on it. It is a gift to the door for what's next.**

If God made us to sit around heaven and praise Him, how vain is He? No, the whole purpose of creation, as I read the Bible, is creative sons, offspring like Him. We think we praise Him with our mouths, that is partly true, but don't we really praise Him through obedience? Isn't imitation the highest form of flattery?

Can God be bought through flattery? If He wanted praise, why didn't He make praise robots?

Romans 2:6 ⁶ He will render to each one <u>according to his works</u>:

Revelation 22:12 ¹² "Behold, I am coming soon, bringing my recompense with me<u>, to repay each one for what he has done</u>.

I see the same people in line for prayer for the same issues week after week. I also noticed about myself that I face the same issues time and time again. After much prayer, I thought I heard, **"There are many reasons, but the most common is you try and come into my presence ungrateful and unclean."**

Psalms 100 ¹ Make a joyful noise unto the LORD, all ye lands. ² <u>Serve the LORD with gladness: come before his presence with singing.</u> ³ Know ye that the LORD he is God: it is he that hath made us, and not we ourselves; we are his people, and the sheep of his pasture. **⁴** Enter into his gates with thanksgiving, and into his courts with praise: be thankful unto him, and bless his name. **⁵** For the LORD is good; his mercy is everlasting; and his truth endureth to all generations.

Matthew 5:23-24 **²³** Therefore if thou bring thy gift to the altar, and there rememberest that thy brother hath ought against thee; **²⁴** Leave there thy gift before the altar, and go thy way; first be reconciled to thy brother, and then come and offer thy gift.

James 4:2-3 **²** Ye lust, and have not: ye kill, and desire to have, and cannot obtain: ye fight and war, yet ye have not, because ye ask not. **³** Ye ask, and receive not, because ye ask amiss, that ye may consume it upon your lusts.

Psalms 24:3-4 **³** Who may ascend into the hill of the LORD? Or who may stand in His holy place? **⁴** He who has clean hands and a pure heart, Who has not lifted up his soul to an idol, Nor sworn deceitfully.

> **Revelation: You can't be peeved and praise Him or enter into His presence with unforgiveness and willful sin. Let it go! (Confess and Repent)**

After having our church for about four years, I was complaining to God about our church not growing. No matter what we did, we never seemed to get above a dozen people. He let me go on for a while. After several weeks I felt the presence of the Holy Spirit and saw a vision of an ocean liner. Then came the question. ***"How long does it take an ocean liner to turn?"*** I replied,

The Ultimate Simulation

"Quite a while, sometimes up to twenty miles". He replied, **"I didn't call you to be an ocean liner. I called you to be a speedboat that will stop, start and turn on my command. Quit comparing yourself to others and do what I tell you".**

On several occasions, nobody came. I was asking if I was missing something, when the Lord said, **"You will never preach to an empty house"**. It sure looked empty to me. In the blink of an eye, I looked beyond the room and saw it was filled with angels. Why do I doubt? Why don't I just trust? Am I that fragile? Do I need constant stroking?

I am going through all of this to show how I got to where the Simulation begins. There is one more story that plays a significant role.

Matthews 24:35 [35] Heaven and earth will pass away, but my words will not pass away.

One of my questions was, if heaven is going to pass away, to what do we aspire? Now I know that many will argue that the heaven referred to is the physical heaven and not to the spiritual one, but I question everything.

For several months I prayed for understanding. One day I was in prayer and had what I would describe as an awake vision. I was completely aware more so than I can ever recall and also aware I was not dreaming. I was suspended in the middle of nowhere. There was nothing. I remember the color of space was like a pale pea soup

The Ultimate Simulation

green. As I looked around I saw two globes. They were connected by a thin glass walkway. The globe on the right was like a giant lava lamp. There was a fire under it that kept things boiling. Colorful blobs where changing and moving. Some ascended while others descended. The other globe was light and calm. People were walking across from turmoil to peace. However, beneath the glass walkway there was a V shaped structure. Anyone who fell off the walkway was caught by this structure and fed into the fire under the first globe. There were not a lot of people making it to the other globe. I watched for a long time. It could have been a second or a year. There was no sense of time. I became aware of something behind me. I turned to see a distant light. How far away it was impossible to determine, except it was very bright and pure. I looked at the light for a long time. As I turned to look back at the globes, they were gone. No noise, no flash of light, no nothing. They had just disappeared. I looked all around, but there was nothing, just this pea soup green.

At this point, I will leave this story and finish it later.

A new question appeared. **"If Jesus only did what he saw the Father do, did he see the Father go to the bathroom?"**

You may think this is sacrilegious, but the issue behind the question is highly relevant. He did things required to live without seeing His Father do them. He had choices.

The Ultimate Simulation

John 5:19 ¹⁹ Then Jesus answered and said to them, "Most assuredly, I say to you, the Son can do nothing of Himself, but what He sees the Father do; for whatever He does, the Son also does in like manner.

> **Revelation: When Jesus saw the Father do something, He did it. In between times, He made Himself available for more through prayer and lived life.**

    I noticed a lot of Christians are afraid of doing something wrong and therefore do nothing. How does God get the glory from slackers? I also realized the most common question among Christians was "What is the will of God in my life?" Over time I developed an answer.

> **Revelation: Unless you have a word from the Lord, do what's in front of you as if unto Him. Do all with quality, zeal, joy and trust.**

    Another question, how is the fear of the Lord the beginning of wisdom?

Proverbs 9:10 ¹⁰ "The fear of the LORD *is* the beginning of wisdom, and the knowledge of the Holy One *is* understanding.

    If I believe the Lord wants me to go over there and between me and there is a snake and I have a fear of snakes. If I fear the snake more than I fear the consequences of not obeying the Lord, then who is God?

The Ultimate Simulation

God doesn't need our worship. He tells us to worship Him because it opens the door to the supernatural.

> **Revelation: Praise and worship are not about what they do for God. They are about what they do for us.**

I had read many different opinions on what the fear of the Lord is. Everyone has an opinion. So I started praying, "Lord, show me the fear of the Lord". After about two months, I had what I call a waking vision. I was in prayer when I was transported to another world. This place was a totally flat plain. In the middle of the plain was a gigantic metal ball. This ball was at least a hundred miles across. It could have been a thousand. I don't know. I was standing very close to the contact point in that I could barely stand upright. I thought, "If this ball moves, I am toast". The ball was so massive I could never out run it. Anyways, there was no place to hide. As I stood there, I felt a vibration start to grow. It grew stronger and stronger. Oh no, the ball was starting to move. I am going to die and there's no escape. The only thing I felt was terror. There was no reverential awe, no sense of judgment, nothing except terror. Then the vision was over. It was so real, I still remember it some twenty years later as if it was yesterday.

Matthew 10:28 ²⁸ And do not fear those who kill the body but cannot kill the soul. But rather <u>fear Him who is able to destroy both soul and body in hell.</u>

The Ultimate Simulation

> **Revelation: We worship what we fear. If God isn't at the top of our fear pyramid, He's not our god.**

Chapter 1: A Pre-Simulation

Being a computer technologist and a puzzle aficionado, I like games that contain puzzles. I especially like simulations. I have learned to stay away from 1st person shooters and violence oriented games as they have an effect on my soul. I have also learned I am subject to addiction.

I remember reading that if Moore's law continued, (double capacity and processing power every 18 months), in about 20-30 years we would have computers with enough memory to simulate every atom in the universe. The first question was, "Has someone already done it?" Followed by, "Are we in it?" I also thought about the Star Trek episode with Moriarty, where he is placed in a simulation.

It was a fun idea and certainly a grand puzzle. I sat on it for years.

In the meantime, I was occupied connecting physical laws with spiritual ones. I reasoned that physical laws had to mimic spiritual ones.

Matthew 5:18 [18] For truly, I say to you, <u>until heaven and earth pass away, not an iota, not a dot, will pass from the Law until all is accomplished</u>.

Matthew 6:10 [10] Your kingdom come, your will be done, <u>on earth as it is in heaven</u>.

These scriptures imply heaven and earth are tied to the Law. If so, there must be common laws.

The Ultimate Simulation

I decided Newton's 1st law of motion was a good place to start.

Newton's 1st law of motion: Things in motion tend to stay in motion; things at rest tend to stay at rest, unless acted upon by an outside force.

What spiritual law was its corollary? I wondered about this for quite a while. It finally occurred to me this could be a description of free will. In other words, without the Holy Spirit, the program running everything is 100% in control. I believe this sets us apart from animals. Free will isn't about normal program choices. What we will eat, what we like and what we choose to do are all program choices and are fixed. These are pseudo-choices that are really controlled by flesh. Our pseudo-choices are a result of survival, comfort, abilities, genetics, experience and opportunity. How we react to the Holy Spirit by faith, determines whether or not we have a destiny of becoming a son. In other words, we have options outside the program. Every time I exercise free will, I must go against the program (flesh).

Romans 8:7-15 ⁷ Because the carnal mind *is* enmity against God; for it is not subject to the law of God, nor indeed can be. ⁸ So then, those who are in the flesh cannot please God. ⁹ But you are not in the flesh but in the Spirit, if indeed the Spirit of God dwells in you. Now if anyone does not have the Spirit of Christ, he is not His. ¹⁰ And if Christ *is* in you, the body *is* dead because of sin, but the Spirit *is* life because of righteousness. ¹¹ But if the Spirit of Him who raised Jesus from the dead dwells in you, He who

The Ultimate Simulation

raised Christ from the dead will also give life to your mortal bodies through His Spirit who dwells in you.

[12] Therefore, brethren, we are debtors—not to the flesh, to live according to the flesh. [13] For if you live according to the flesh you will die; but if by the Spirit you put to death the deeds of the body, you will live. [14] <u>For as many as are led by the Spirit of God, these are sons of God</u>. [15] For you did not receive the spirit of bondage again to fear, but you received the Spirit of adoption by whom we cry out, "Abba, Father."

I developed the following illustration about God's first law of motion.

Suppose you developed a two dimensional world. Everyone coming into the world was born with a specific velocity and vector. The physical laws would try and keep them moving along the same vector at the same speed.

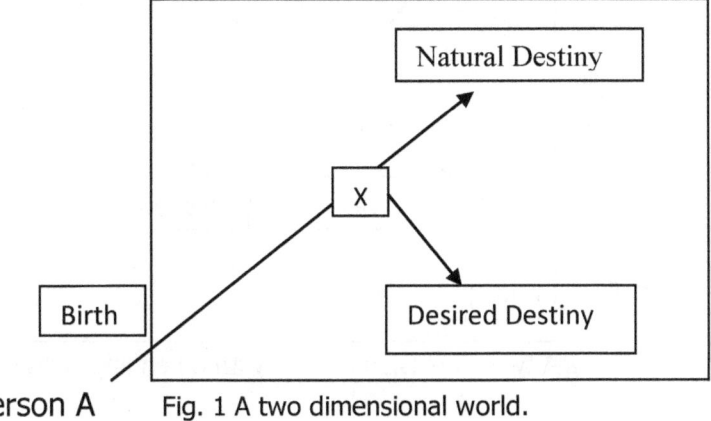

Person A   Fig. 1 A two dimensional world.

This would be the case if there were no other 2 dimensional objects or people. But as the creator of the

The Ultimate Simulation

world, you realize that the best for person A would be the Desired Destiny. How do I influence them without direct intervention, negating their free will? So I whisper in their ear, "Turn right at point X". If they have never learned to hear my voice, then when everything in them tells them to continue straight, they will continue straight as the law of motion tells them.

John 10:27 [27] <u>My sheep hear My voice</u>, and I know them, and they follow Me.

Now I insert person B, who is a bus driver, into the world. I do the math and see that in 2 weeks there will be an accident. So I whisper in the ear of person A, "Turn left at Y".

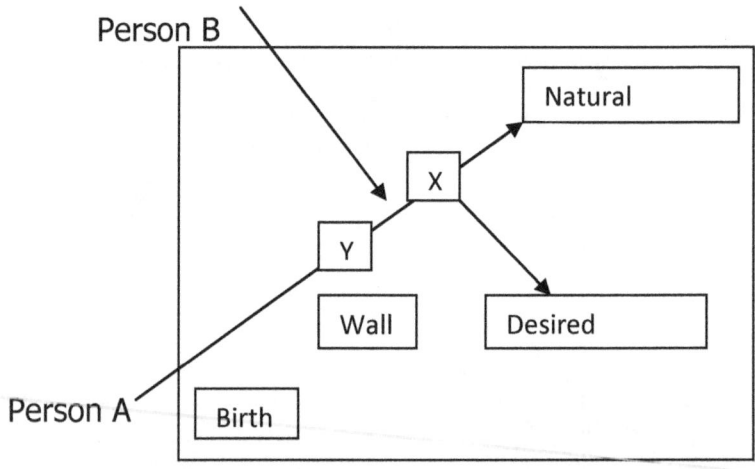

Fig. 2 A two dimensional world with a pending collision.

Suppose I had already showed person A in a dream the Desired Destiny. Turning left makes no sense, because my destiny is to the right. But what they can't see is a wall

The Ultimate Simulation

to their right that would stop them. The whole point is that this world is a mine field and there are billions of interactions. By being led by the Spirit to do what is counterintuitive is what faith is.

A faith walk may look like this.

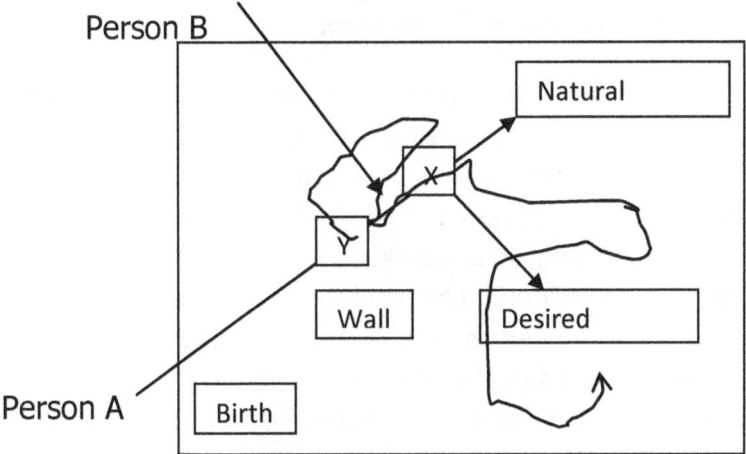

Fig. 3 A two dimensional world showing the best possible way to reach the Desired Destiny.

Each time we exercise our free will and follow the Holy Spirit, we sweep through a myriad of possible futures until we stop turning, at which point our future again becomes fixed. Will you give up a natural destiny for a Spirit led God Desired Destiny?

Revelation: Faith and the God kind of love are both spelled "RISK". If it's easy and doesn't go against my flesh, it probably isn't faith.

The Ultimate Simulation

Think of flesh or selfishness as programmed responses. The Biblical Law was given to tell us what program responses will be blessings and which ones will be curses.

Whenever we ask for more of something, like faith, what God says is **"Okay, I'll put you in a situation where more faith is required."**

Ouch! When it comes to faith and the fruit of the Spirit, I learned not to ask for more, but to maximize what I have been given. Only a brave soul would ever pray for more patience. I know someone who did and the result nearly killed him. In a few weeks everything in his life he counted on changed. Lost his job. Wife threatened to leave. Children became rebellious... It took months for his life to regain a semblance of order. Although after everything died down, he had more patience. Count the cost.

Galatians 5:22-25 [22] But the fruit of the Spirit is love, joy, peace, longsuffering, kindness, goodness, faithfulness, [23] gentleness, self-control. <u>Against such there is no law</u>. [24] And those *who are* Christ's have crucified the flesh with its passions and desires. [25] <u>If we live in the Spirit, let us also walk in the Spirit.</u>

One day I was asking the Lord about something that I wasn't having victory over. He replied **"Why are you kind to evil"?**

The Ultimate Simulation

I was always told to be kind to everyone. I didn't like evil, but I didn't hate it. I had often joked "Lord, keep me from temptation, but not too far."

Psalms 97:10 [10] O you who love the LORD, hate evil! He preserves the lives of his saints; he delivers them from the hand of the wicked.

> **Revelation: You cannot be kind to your own failings and expect victory over them.**

Jesus was not what we would call a kind man. The truth always came first, along with the most effective way of communicating His point. He was not kind to religious leaders who abused the people, but He was kind to children.

2 Corinthians 10:4-6 [4] For the weapons of our warfare are not of the flesh but have divine power to destroy strongholds. [5] We destroy arguments and every lofty opinion raised against the knowledge of God, and take every thought captive to obey Christ, [6] being ready to punish every disobedience, when your obedience is complete.

> **Revelation: You can't be a part-time or fair weather warrior. You career as a warrior will be short if you don't have substantial prayer support.**

When I excuse my own problems to being human, I am reminded I am not human. I'm a child of God. There's no place to hide, like Adam. One day I heard,

The Ultimate Simulation

"The only way to succeed is to consider yourself a resident alien".

We have not been called to a conventional ministry. We are pioneers for the Kingdom. Most of the church does not understand why we aren't like them. As a result, we are warriors and have had to develop a thick skin. Some things the Lord says, I cannot talk about. If I don't understand, how can I communicate it? If we didn't have visions about our destiny, we would have quit long ago.

We visited a friend's church that was having a prophet and his wife minister. We were hoping for a word, but it seemed everyone around us was getting one except us. Finally they called us up. We got what I would call a generic bless you word. I don't remember anything said. We were heading back to our seat when the prophet's wife said "Sir, the Lord is saying He's giving you great peace." I turned around and said "Thank you." She said "You don't understand. The Lord is giving you great peace". I replied another "Thank you". She said, "You really don't understand. The Lord is giving you great peace". Now she had my attention. I looked at her intently and said "Okay". Two days later I lost my job and went into a season where everything in our life changed. It took about eight months to get everything resolved, but through it I had great peace. Maybe I don't need to go out of my way to get a prophetic word.

The Ultimate Simulation

> **Revelation: God doesn't give you anything that you're not required to use. Be careful what you ask for. Count the cost.**

There are three voices in our head.

1. Our natural mind (flesh) is the loudest.

(Feed me. Doesn't she look good? I won't get caught speeding.)

2. The enemy, spiritual wickedness in high places. (God will forgive you. Did God really say...?)

3. The Holy Spirit is the softest.

(Don't go there. Isn't it prayer time? Tell that person Jesus loves them.)

1 Kings 19:11-12 [11] And he said, Go forth, and stand upon the mount before the LORD. And, behold, the LORD passed by, and a great and strong wind rent the mountains, and brake in pieces the rocks before the LORD; but the LORD was not in the wind: and after the wind an earthquake; but the LORD was not in the earthquake: [12] And after the earthquake a fire; but the LORD was not in the fire: and <u>after the fire a still small voice.</u>

Jeremiah 29:11 [11] For I know the thoughts that I think toward you, says the LORD, thoughts of peace and not of evil, to give you a future and a hope.

The Ultimate Simulation

The difference between the sons of God and humankind is the Holy Spirit along with DNA, RNA and blood changes. I believe the more committed we are to Christ; the more physical changes are made to our bodies. There is something about the blood.

Genesis 2:7 ⁷ And the LORD God formed man *of* the dust of the ground, and breathed into his nostrils the breath of life; and man became a living being.

Nothing is said whether God used an existing pattern for his potential sons or a totally new design. It appears humankind already existed. Without the Breath of God, which is the Holy Spirit, we exist, but don't live because we have no future. Living without a future or without purpose is existing.

After Cain killed Abel there is this.

Genesis 4:14-17 ¹⁴ Behold, you have driven me today away from the ground, and from your face I shall be hidden. I shall be a fugitive and a wanderer on the earth and whoever finds me will kill me." ¹⁵ Then the LORD said to him, "Not so! If anyone kills Cain, vengeance shall be taken on him sevenfold." And the LORD put a mark on Cain, lest any who found him should attack him. ¹⁶ Then Cain went away from the presence of the LORD and settled in the land of Nod, east of Eden. ¹⁷ Cain knew his wife, and she conceived and bore Enoch. When he built a city, he called the name of the city after the name of his son, Enoch.

Where did the people in the land of Nod come from? Where did enough people to warrant a city come from?

The Ultimate Simulation

An interesting note: The word for Adam in Hebrew can mean mankind or be a proper name.

What happened when Adam fell? Was Adam a race, an individual or both? Were there Adams that didn't fall?

So it appears that it was always God's plan that Adam would fall.

Genesis 2:9 ⁹ And out of the ground made the LORD God to grow every tree that is pleasant to the sight, and good for food; <u>the tree of life also in the midst of the garden, and the tree of knowledge of good and evil.</u>

It was God that planted the tree of knowledge of good and evil. And it appears that Adam didn't know evil. In a prophetic sense, Jesus could be the tree of life and the Law could be the tree of the knowledge of good and evil.

Revelation 13:8 ⁸ And all that dwell upon the earth shall worship him, <u>whose names are not written in the book of life of the Lamb slain from the foundation of the world.</u>

This does not mean that the Lamb was slain at the foundation of the world, but that it was always the plan from the foundation that He would be. This means Adam had to eat of the tree of the knowledge of good and evil and fall. In order to become one of God's offspring he had to know good and evil. Adam had to learn to choose by faith to rise above the program and evil. Adam had to be separated from God to make this choice.

The Ultimate Simulation

> **Revelation: In order to be in the Sonship class of beings we go away from the mind of flesh and towards the mind of God through the Holy Spirit and His attributes of love, mercy and grace.**

Genesis 3:22 [22] And the LORD God said, <u>Behold, the man is become as one of us, to know good and evil:</u> and now, lest he put forth his hand, and take also of the tree of life, and eat, and live forever:

Romans 8:20 [20] <u>For the creature was made subject to vanity, not willingly,</u> but by reason of him who hath subjected the same in hope,

So vanity and pride were built into creation deliberately. I am of the opinion God may not have known the exact moment Adam would fall, but He knew he eventually would.

Here we see why mercy, grace and a Messiah are part of the plan. Once fallen, there was no way back. And because the cards were stacked against us, there had to be a way to mitigate and overcome the program laws. I believe the same is true for Lucifer. The fall of Lucifer and Adam was in the math. Except for Lucifer there is no way back.

The Messiah is the unilateral action of God to provide a means of redemption from the law. Mercy is not giving us what we deserve. Grace is giving us something we don't deserve. However, mercy and grace are only available to those who by faith seek Him. Failure doesn't

The Ultimate Simulation

bother God, quitting and lack of faith does. As long as we are trying by faith, His mercy and grace are ever present.

Are there things not covered by mercy and grace?

> **Revelation: Disobedience of any of His commandments without confession and rebellion in any form, which includes unforgiveness and unrepentance, are not covered by mercy and grace.**

Mark 11:26 ²⁶ But <u>if you do not forgive, neither will your Father in heaven forgive your trespasses</u>.

1 John 1:9 ⁹ <u>If we confess our sins, He is faithful and just to forgive us *our* sins</u> and to cleanse us from all unrighteousness.

According to the above verses, forgiveness is conditional. We can activate mercy by confessing our sins and forgiving, but it isn't automatic.

Romans 10:17 ¹⁷ So then <u>faith *comes* by hearing, and hearing by the word of God</u>.

This is not just hearing the spoken Word, but the Word of God revealed to me by the Spirit.

Some time ago I heard the Lord say ***"Quit trying to do my job. Let the Word do the work."***

I was confusing "Doing the Word" with trying to make things happen. Because of my lack of faith I was trying to help things along. Forgive me Father.

The Ultimate Simulation

Isaiah 55:10-11 [10] "For as the rain and the snow come down from heaven and do not return there but water the earth, making it bring forth and sprout, giving seed to the sower and bread to the eater, [11] <u>so shall my word be that goes out from my mouth; it shall not return to me empty, but it shall accomplish that which I purpose, and shall succeed in the thing for which I sent it.</u>

> **Revelation: Embedded in the revelation or assignment from God is the required power enabled by faith to accomplish it.**

A side note. In infinity logic, anything that has a probability greater than zero exists now. Maybe certain things only appear to have a probability of zero because of my perspective.

> **Revelation: Truth is a point. Reality is my perspective of the point. The more perspectives I have, the closer I get to understanding the whole truth. The closer I get to the truth, the harder it gets to change perspective. Catch 22?**

In Genesis, God makes an amazing statement at the tower of Babel.

Genesis 11:5-6 [5] But the LORD came down to see the city and the tower which the sons of men had built. [6] And the LORD said, "Indeed the people *are* one and they all have one language, and this is what they begin to do; <u>now nothing that they propose to do will be withheld from them.</u>

The Ultimate Simulation

Question: If God is omnipresent, the way most people think, why did He need to come down and see what men were doing?

Possibilities are built into this creation. I believe in the tower of Babel story God directly intervened to disrupt because it would have interfered with His end-game. However, these possibilities came about through unity (resonance).

The mystery of unity and one flesh is for another time.

Chapter 2: A Simulation

Now the big question of this book. Are we living in a simulation? Before we can come to any conclusions, we need to explore various aspects of this reality and see how they fit into a simulation while maintaining the truth of God's Word.

I have included scripture verses because most people reading this will probably not know them or wouldn't look them up. Also, I am not a big fan of certain translations.

Chapter 3: The Purpose of the Simulation

Anything created has a purpose. So what does the Bible say about purpose.

John 1:12-13 [12] But to all who did receive him, who believed in his name, he gave the right to become children of God, [13] who were born, not of blood nor of the will of the flesh nor of the will of man, but of God.

Genesis 1:26 [26] Then God said, "Let us make man in our image, after our likeness. And let them have dominion over the fish of the sea and over the birds of the heavens and over the livestock and over all the earth and over every creeping thing that creeps on the earth."

Genesis 1:28 [28] And God blessed them. And God said to them, "Be fruitful and multiply and fill the earth and subdue it, and have dominion over the fish of the sea and over the birds of the heavens and over every living thing that moves on the earth."

Romans 8:29 [29] For those whom he foreknew he also predestined to be conformed to the image of his Son, in order that he might be the firstborn among many brothers.

Jeremiah 30:22 [22] And you shall be my people, and I will be your God.

Romans 12:2 [2] Do not be conformed to this world, but be transformed by the renewal of your mind, that by testing you may discern what is the will of God, what is good and acceptable and perfect.

The Ultimate Simulation

There are a lot more scriptures, but this is sufficient for now.

I believe the first chapter of Genesis lays out the purpose and plan for this creation. (Offspring and dominion). Later on He clarifies offspring as those who believe on Him and do His will. And finally to offspring that does the prior and submits to a transformation process via an active relationship with Him via the Holy Spirit.

There are many Christians that believe the knowledge of how creation works is beyond our understanding. I don't. In order to have dominion, I need to know. Adam being able to name every creature implies an overwhelming knowledge of nature, as name follows function.

In order to fulfill the purpose (will) of God I need the potential capacity to accomplish it. Is it automatic? No, I have to work for it and pursue it. This doesn't mean I am equal with God, but that I have authority and ability from God for things over which I am given dominion. Dominion doesn't only mean to rule over, but to also explore possibilities and maximize what's been given's potential. Think about the parable of the talents.

Matthew 25:14-30 [14] "For *the kingdom of heaven is like a man traveling to a far country, who* called his own servants and delivered his goods to them. [15] And to one he gave five talents, to another two, and to another one, to each according to his own ability; and immediately he went on a journey. [16] Then he who had received the five talents went and traded with them, and made another five talents.

The Ultimate Simulation

¹⁷ And likewise he who *had received* two gained two more also. ¹⁸ But he who had received one went and dug in the ground, and hid his lord's money. ¹⁹ After a long time the lord of those servants came and settled accounts with them.

²⁰ "So he who had received five talents came and brought five other talents, saying, 'Lord, you delivered to me five talents; look, I have gained five more talents besides them.' ²¹ His lord said to him, 'Well *done,* good and faithful servant; you were faithful over a few things, I will make you ruler over many things. Enter into the joy of your lord.' 22 He also who had received two talents came and said, 'Lord, you delivered to me two talents; look, I have gained two more talents besides them.' ²³ His lord said to him, 'Well *done,* good and faithful servant; you have been faithful over a few things, I will make you ruler over many things. Enter into the joy of your lord.'

²⁴ "Then he who had received the one talent came and said, 'Lord, I knew you to be a hard man, reaping where you have not sown, and gathering where you have not scattered seed. ²⁵ And I was afraid, and went and hid your talent in the ground. Look, *there* you have *what is* yours.'

²⁶ "But his lord answered and said to him, '<u>You wicked and lazy servant, you knew that I reap where I have not sown, and gather where I have not scattered seed.</u> ²⁷ <u>So you ought to have deposited my money with the bankers, and at my coming I would have received back my own with interest.</u> ²⁸ <u>So take the talent from him, and give</u> *it* <u>to him who has ten talents.</u>

²⁹ 'For to everyone who has, more will be given, and he will have abundance; but from him who does not have, even what he has will be taken away. ³⁰ And cast the

The Ultimate Simulation

unprofitable servant into the outer darkness. There will be weeping and gnashing of teeth.'

Usually all Christians believe what God says about Jesus, but sadly most Christians don't believe what God says about them. The Lord said **"Why do you ask me to do what I have given you authority over? You have reached the age of accountability."**

Exodus 14:13-16 [13] And Moses said unto the people, Fear ye not, stand still, and see the salvation of the LORD, which he will shew to you to day: for the Egyptians whom ye have seen to day, ye shall see them again no more for ever. [14] The LORD shall fight for you, and ye shall hold your peace. [15] And the LORD said unto Moses, Wherefore criest thou unto me? speak unto the children of Israel, that they go forward: [16] But lift thou up thy rod, and stretch out thine hand over the sea, and divide it: and the children of Israel shall go on dry ground through the midst of the sea.

In other words I believe the Lord was saying to Moses, **"Why are you asking me to do what I have given you authority over? Don't you believe that what I have given you is sufficient for the task? You lift your rod and you part the sea."**

> **Revelation: God didn't part the Red Sea. Moses did, using the authority God had given him.**

I believe we become accountable when we move from the milk of the Word to the meat.

Hebrews 5:12-14 [12] For though by this time you ought to be teachers, you need *someone* to teach you again the

The Ultimate Simulation

first principles of the oracles of God; and you have come to need milk and not solid food. <u>[13] For everyone who partakes *only* of milk *is* unskilled in the word of righteousness, for he is a babe.</u> [14] But solid food belongs to those who are of full age, *that is,* those who by reason of use have their senses exercised to discern both good and evil.

Shouldn't those who are of full age be doing the following?

Matthew 10:7-8 [7] And as ye go, preach, saying, The kingdom of heaven is at hand. <u>[8] Heal the sick, cleanse the lepers, raise the dead, cast out devils: freely ye have received, freely give.</u>

> **Revelation: If we are who we say we are then why aren't we doing what He says we can?**

If you are trying to reach a destination or understanding that is either beyond your capability or off-limits, He will let you know. If you haven't reached that limit there are unexplored possibilities you're leaving undeveloped. Get out of your comfort zone and explore possibilities. Be creative, but stay within the bounds of His Word. Just remember, He gets all the glory.

Matthew 19:26 [26] But Jesus looked at them and said, <u>"With man this is impossible, but with God all things are possible."</u>

What this is saying is if we are tuned into His will, there isn't anything His will allows that is impossible for us.

The Ultimate Simulation

That includes wisdom and knowledge. 'All things' does not include anything that contradicts His Word.

> **Revelation: First become obedient to and proficient in what His Word commands. Then you can proceed into what His Word allows.**

James 1:5-6 ⁵ If any of you lacks wisdom, let him ask of God, who gives to all liberally and without reproach, and it will be given to him. ⁶ But let him ask in faith, with no doubting, for he who doubts is like a wave of the sea driven and tossed by the wind.

Psalms 37:4-5 ⁴ Delight yourself also in the LORD, And He shall give you the desires of your heart. ⁵ Commit your way to the LORD, Trust also in Him, And He shall bring *it* to pass.

It is not my desire to know everything, live forever or be saved. It is my desire to become what and who He hopes I will. Possessing everything He says I can have. He will reward me in due season according to my faithfulness. I believe God has said to me, **"Show Me you are one of mine and surprise me with possibilities."**

Are we, in a sense, a reality show for God? Not that it is His main purpose, but a side benefit by making Him laugh.

Psalms 2:1-4 ¹ Why do the nations rage,
And the people plot a vain thing?
² The kings of the earth set themselves,

The Ultimate Simulation

And the rulers take counsel together,
Against the LORD and against His Anointed, *saying,*
³ "Let us break Their bonds in pieces
And cast away Their cords from us."

<u>⁴ He who sits in the heavens shall laugh;
The Lord shall hold them in derision.</u>

Chapter 4: The Nature of God

The basis for Christianity is one God in three persons. (Father, Son and Holy Spirit). This is how He describes himself.

Deuteronomy 6:4 ⁴ "Hear, O Israel: The LORD our God, the LORD is one.

1Corinthians 12:4-6 ⁴ Now there are varieties of gifts, but the same Spirit; ⁵ and there are varieties of service, but the same Lord; ⁶ and there are varieties of activities, but it is the same God who empowers them all in everyone.

Matthew 24:36 ³⁶ "But concerning that day and hour no one knows, not even the angels of heaven, nor the Son, but the Father only.

This one in three parts is a repeating pattern. The top three are:

1. Father, Son and Holy Spirit
2. Mind, will and emotion
3. Body, soul and spirit

Body, soul and spirit are how we interact with this reality. They are not the image of God. Mind, will and emotion are.

The Ultimate Simulation

To summarize:

> Father is in charge of purpose and time
>
> Son is in charge of creation and matter
>
> Holy Spirit is in charge of supernatural power and drawing people to the Father

Scripture usually categorizes them as the will of the Father, the mind of Christ and the power of the Holy Spirit.

John 1:18 [18] No one has seen God at any time. The only begotten Son, who is in the bosom of the Father, He has declared *Him.*

I don't know of any particular reason God would describe Himself as triune except if it is possibly a key to understanding this creation through reverse engineering. Likewise in the description of the throne and its surroundings.

The reader may not be familiar with programming/computer ideas. Here is a possible very high overview of this simulations software architecture.

The Ultimate Simulation

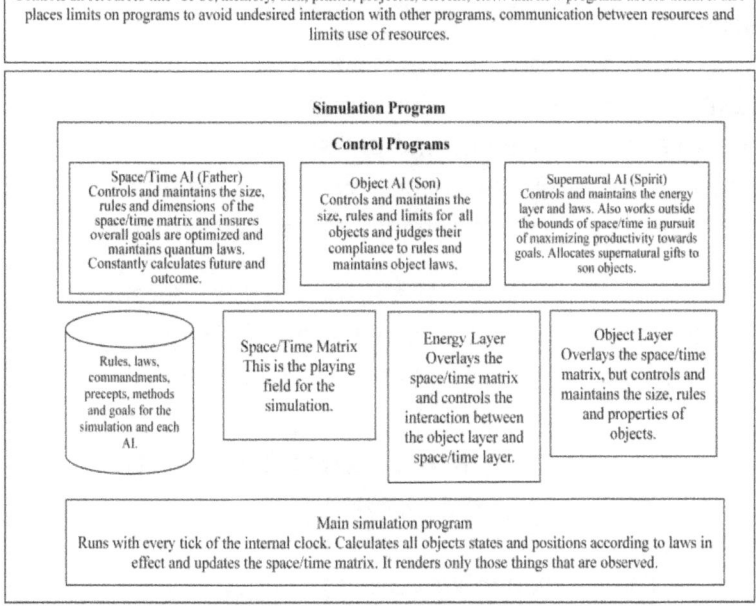

Fig. 4 High level diagram of simulation software architecture.

In the simulation, this idea of trinity is repeated in the control program with three sections, each with its own artificial intelligence (AI).

1. Father AI which oversees the time/space matrix and forecasts the future to insure the goals are met and prophecies fulfilled.

2. The Son AI that oversees the architecture and management of the simulation to optimize the Fathers goals, compliance to the Fathers laws and judges the completeness of each object.

The Ultimate Simulation

3. The Spirit AI that oversees supernatural power distributions to optimize the Fathers goals as He sees fit.

In case you are wondering, I've characterized human beings as objects for simulation purposes. When we accept Jesus we become pre-son objects which are a similar class as human objects with extra properties and methods. Jesus will determine our final classification.

This reminds me of a spiritual truth. Because spiritual anointings are distributed as the Holy Spirit sees fit, then anointings are not an endorsement of character.

> **Revelation: A jerk with anointing is still a jerk. Respect the anointing.**

The simulation was designed to produce object AIs that emulated the characteristics as set forth in the rules.

Romans 8:29 ^{29} For those whom he foreknew he also predestined to be conformed to the image of his Son, in order that he might <u>be the firstborn among many brothers</u>.

Ephesians 1:19-21 ^{19} and what is the immeasurable greatness of his power toward us who believe, according to the working of his great might ^{20} that he worked in Christ when he raised him from the dead and seated him at his right hand in the heavenly places, ^{21} far above all rule and authority and power and dominion, and above every name that is named, not only in this age but also in the one to come.

Question: What happens after the age to come?

The Ultimate Simulation

> **Simulation Conclusion: Jesus was the first born who became the Christ after His design and management of this simulation and took His position in The Son AI to which in the future other Sons will be added.**

It's time to address another problem. Most Christians believe and confess that God is in control. By implication, then everything that happens is engineered by Him both good and evil. I believe God runs the simulation, and the events and conditions of the simulation are the result of the simulation rules and interactions, not God engineering them. The only time God inserts Himself into the simulation directly is when His end-game is put in jeopardy or in the fulfillment of appointed times.

God did not cause your loved one to get cancer and die, nor did He cause your child to be still born. In the simulation good and bad happens. The Holy Spirit tries to draw us and adds power when there is faith. God warns us if we do 'this' good things will happen and if we don't or do 'that' bad things will occur. These are the rules of the simulation interacting with trillions of objects and people.

Romans 2:11 [11] For there is no partiality with God.

Acts 10:34 [34] Then Peter opened his mouth, and said, Of a truth I perceive that God is no respecter of persons:

The Ultimate Simulation

Matthew 5:45 [45] that you may be sons of your Father in heaven; <u>for He makes His sun rise on the evil and on the good, and sends rain on the just and on the unjust.</u>

    In most cases, when people say "God is in control or God can do anything.", they are really expressing doubt and unbelief concerning their own responsibility to be doers of the word and not hearers only and or recipients of bad teaching. What they are really saying is "God doesn't need me or I am unwilling to go." I have a tendency to over explain. In this case I want you to think of possibilities about what this means. My revelations are for me. They may be universally true. You decide if they are real for you.

> **Simulation Revelation: This entire creation/simulation was for the development of possibilities each of us possess in Him. When a person is lost, their possibilities are lost.**

Chapter 5: One-Trick Ponies

I wrote this several years ago and am including it because it gives insight into the uncertainty factor.

I don't know when it started, but as long as I can remember, I've been a proponent of principal and process over facts. There are any number of ways to interpret a fact. Which way is correct is always conjecture unless it can be shown to be part of a bigger picture. After all, a fact is just a snapshot of circumstances that appears to be repeatable. In any possible solution to the theory of everything, there will always be an almost infinite number of one-trick ponies. If the one-trick pony is a deemed a fact, then one can never comprehend a process whose sole purpose is to produce them. Science is the effort to correlate one-trick ponies. Of course every now and then one of these exhibits another trick which causes a meltdown in the scientific community. Is this really another trick or is it merely another aspect of the first trick that has yet to be explored? If the one-trick ponies are unique, then one can never exactly equal one. It can only approximate it. I don't know who originated this, but ... "For every problem in the universe, no matter how complex, there is a simple, readily understood answer, that won't quite work." There is no scientific solution for the unique one-trick pony universe, only an approximation. And while exponential in nature, it can never quite get there.

A philosopher might be able to bridge the gap, but there would always be that uncertainty. If the one-trick

The Ultimate Simulation

ponies are self directed with a latent ability to alter circumstances, then each pony would have the potential of having their own uncertainty factor. While most never discover it, the ones that do wreak havoc with science. Science is only king in a completely fatalistic universe.

What are the clues we aren't living in a fatalistic universe? I guess the place to start would be looking at the world's religions. All mainstream religions are fatalistic except Christianity. By fatalistic I mean they represent a linear progression of development resulting in a final objective. In other words, I can work my way to God. Christianity has at its heart a non-fatalistic premise. I can affect my destination not by what I achieve, but what I commit to. Also, there is no way to progressively attain nirvana or ascension. Christianity has the requirement that one reject fatalism. However, modern Christianity is almost totally fatalistic. Church leaders and scholars have rejected non-fatalism in exchange for political correctness and as rational for the absence of change in their own lives. In doing so, they have exchanged the religions promise with the one fate provides.

Let's look then at what Christianity says about fate. We will take the Bible's most famous passage, John 3:16 and see what it says. In order to get a bigger picture lets place the passage in context. The theme starts in verse one and continues through verse 21.

John 3:1-21 [1] There was a man of the Pharisees named Nicodemus, a ruler of the Jews. [2] This man came to Jesus by night and said to Him, "Rabbi, we know that You are a

The Ultimate Simulation

teacher come from God; for no one can do these signs that You do unless God is with him."

³ Jesus answered and said to him, "Most assuredly, I say to you, unless one is born again, he cannot see the kingdom of God."

⁴ Nicodemus said to Him, "How can a man be born when he is old? Can he enter a second time into his mother's womb and be born?"

⁵ Jesus answered, "Most assuredly, I say to you, unless one is born of water and the Spirit, he cannot enter the kingdom of God. ⁶ That which is born of the flesh is flesh, and that which is born of the Spirit is spirit. ⁷ Do not marvel that I said to you, 'You must be born again.' ⁸ <u>The wind blows where it wishes, and you hear the sound of it, but cannot tell where it comes from and where it goes. So is everyone who is born of the Spirit.</u>"

⁹ Nicodemus answered and said to Him, "How can these things be?"

¹⁰ Jesus answered and said to him, "Are you the teacher of Israel, and do not know these things? ¹¹ Most assuredly, I say to you, We speak what We know and testify what We have seen, and you do not receive Our witness. ¹² If I have told you earthly things and you do not believe, how will you believe if I tell you heavenly things? ¹³ No one has ascended to heaven but He who came down from heaven, *that is,* the Son of Man who is in heaven. ¹⁴ And as Moses lifted up the serpent in the wilderness, even so must the Son of Man be lifted up, ¹⁵ that whoever believes in Him should not perish but have eternal life. ¹⁶ <u>For God so loved the world that He gave His only begotten Son, that whoever</u>

The Ultimate Simulation

<u>believes in Him should not perish but have everlasting life.</u>
[17] For God did not send His Son into the world to condemn the world, but that the world through Him might be saved.

18 "He who believes in Him is not condemned; but he who does not believe is condemned already, because he has not believed in the name of the only begotten Son of God. [19] And this is the condemnation, that the light has come into the world, and men loved darkness rather than light, because their deeds were evil. [20] For everyone practicing evil hates the light and does not come to the light, lest his deeds should be exposed. [21] <u>But he who does the truth comes to the light, that his deeds may be clearly seen, that they have been done in God.</u>"

It's both interesting and pathetic that a spiritual leader came to Jesus by night and says that Jesus must be from God because it appears He does not operate under the same set of rules that they do (miracles). In other words, they recognized that Jesus was not bound by fatalism as they were. It's amazing how many fatalists there are in the church, who recognize when the way of flesh is superseded, yet deny it as possible for them or anyone under their oversight. (They also always say that God can do anything which demonstrates an infantile understanding of Him and Scripture).

God is not fully sovereign, His Word is. (Since He cannot violate His Word, His Word is sovereign, although He could issue a new Word that is not at odds with His existing Word.). Having His Word or rules be sovereign strongly points to a simulation with rule based control.

The Ultimate Simulation

Jesus' response to this statement is that one must be born again or from above to be able <u>to see</u> the kingdom of God. In His response I believe He is stating that a release of the spirit is required to see beyond the way of flesh.

Chapter 6: The Soul

A number of years ago, I was praying about what I could use as an analogy for the soul. What I received was a picture of a pewter plate. I'll call this a blank. Everything we say, think and do is recorded on this blank. When we are obedient to what God is doing and leading then patches of gold and silver are pressed into the plate. At the end of our life, all plates go through the fire. At this point, the pewter reflows covering everything except the gold and silver. If I had gold and silver and then renounced God, the gold and silver are cut out. In the end, if there is no gold or silver, the plate returns blank and all its information is in essence left in the fire. If the plate is blank, it is available for recycle. Only plates that retain information are keepers.

Malachi 4:1 [1] "For behold, the day is coming, Burning like an oven, And all the proud, yes, all who do wickedly will be stubble. <u>And the day which is coming shall burn them up</u>," Says the LORD of hosts, "That will leave them neither root nor branch.

1 Corinthians 3:11-17 [11] For no other foundation can anyone lay than that which is laid, which is Jesus Christ. [12] Now if anyone builds on this foundation *with* gold, silver, precious stones, wood, hay, straw, [13] each one's work will become clear; for the Day will declare it, <u>because it will be revealed by fire; and the fire will test each one's work, of what sort it is.</u> [14] <u>If anyone's work which he has built on *it* endures, he will receive a reward.</u> [15] <u>If anyone's work is burned, he will suffer loss</u>; but he himself will be saved, yet so as through fire. [16] Do you not know that you are the

The Ultimate Simulation

temple of God and *that* the Spirit of God dwells in you? ¹⁷ If anyone defiles the temple of God, God will destroy him. For the temple of God is holy, which *temple* you are.

Hebrews 4:12 ¹² For the word of God *is* living and powerful, and sharper than any two-edged sword, <u>piercing even to the division of soul and spirit</u>, and of joints and marrow, and is a discerner of the thoughts and intents of the heart.

Both analogies, joints and marrow, and soul and spirit, are of something encased in another. In other words, the word of God frees the marrow from the bone and frees the spirit from the soul. This is a type for birth, the freeing of life from the shell. The Greek word for "word" in this passage is logos, the same term used by John when referring to Jesus. Jesus is the discerner of hearts and is the only way to free the spirit from the prison of soul.

Another interesting insight is the Greek word for soul here is psuche, pronounced psoo-khay. In the garden after Adam and Eve ate of the forbidden fruit, their eyes were opened and they saw they were naked and clothed themselves with fig leaves. The Greek word for fig tree is suke, pronounced soo-kay. Is this a deliberate homonym?

Could it be that Adam and Eve entered so completely into soul as to think they could hide their spirit from God inside their soul? So the work of Satan was knowing he could not defeat the spirit of the man, tricked

The Ultimate Simulation

him into leaving his birthright in the spirit for the pleasures and reasoning's of the soul.

This leads us to:

1 John 3:8 [8] He who sins is of the devil, for the devil has sinned from the beginning. <u>For this purpose the Son of God was manifested, that He might destroy the works of the devil.</u>

So Jesus, the Word, is the key to the breaking of the soul for the release of the spirit and rebirth. Without this rebirth we cannot see the kingdom of God. The breaking of the soul only occurs with a fracturing of the heart. Heart is a type for soul not spirit. People led by their heart are unstable and soulish. People led by their mind are equally soulish although they are usually more stable.

Matthew 12:34 [34] Brood of vipers! How can you, being evil, speak good things? <u>For out of the abundance of the heart the mouth speaks.</u>

So the mouth doesn't speak anything that isn't in the heart. So the tongue is the window of the soul.

Mark 7:20-23 [20] And He said, "<u>What comes out of a man, that defiles a man.</u> [21] For from within, out of the heart of men, proceed evil thoughts, adulteries, fornications, murders, [22] thefts, covetousness, wickedness, deceit, lewdness, an evil eye, blasphemy, pride, foolishness. [23] <u>All these evil things come from within and defile a man.</u>"

Joel 2:12:13 [12] "Now, therefore," says the LORD, "Turn to Me with all your heart, With fasting, with weeping, and with mourning." [13] So <u>rend your heart, and not your</u>

The Ultimate Simulation

<u>garments</u>; Return to the LORD your God, For He *is* gracious and merciful, Slow to anger, and of great kindness; And He relents from doing harm.

Joel admonishes us to break our hearts. (Fracture our soul for the release of the spirit). The breech only comes from true repentance and forgiveness. Saying you're sorry isn't repentance. True repentance is reflected by change. Repentance literally means to turn and go in the opposite direction. Likewise, true forgiveness does not seek vengeance or punishment. True forgiveness refuses to judge and releases all claims for punishment.

James 3:1-10 ¹ My brethren, let not many of you become teachers, knowing that we shall receive a stricter judgment. ² For we all stumble in many things. <u>If anyone does not stumble in word, he *is* a perfect man, able also to bridle the whole body.</u> ³ Indeed, we put bits in horses' mouths that they may obey us, and we turn their whole body. ⁴ Look also at ships: although they are so large and are driven by fierce winds, they are turned by a very small rudder wherever the pilot desires. ⁵ Even so the tongue is a little member and boasts great things.

See how great a forest a little fire kindles! ⁶ <u>And the tongue *is* a fire, a world of iniquity. The tongue is so set among our members that it defiles the whole body, and sets on fire the course of nature; and it is set on fire by hell.</u> ⁷ For every kind of beast and bird, of reptile and creature of the sea, is tamed and has been tamed by mankind. ⁸ But no man can tame the tongue. *It is* an unruly evil, full of deadly poison. ⁹ With it we bless our God and Father, and with it we curse men, who have been made in the similitude of

The Ultimate Simulation

God. <u>¹⁰ Out of the same mouth proceed blessing and cursing. My brethren, these things ought not to be so.</u>

He, who controls his tongue, controls his heart (soul) which in its natural state is evil.

Matthew 16:13-19 ¹³ When Jesus came into the region of Caesarea Philippi, He asked His disciples, saying, "Who do men say that I, the Son of Man, am?" ¹⁴ So they said, "Some *say* John the Baptist, some Elijah, and others Jeremiah or one of the prophets." ¹⁵ He said to them, <u>"But who do you say that I am?"</u> ¹⁶ Simon Peter answered and said, "You are the Christ, the Son of the living God."

¹⁷ Jesus answered and said to him, "Blessed are you, Simon Bar-Jonah, for flesh and blood has not revealed *this* to you, but My Father who is in heaven. ¹⁸ And I also say to you that you are Peter, and on this rock I will build My church, and the gates of Hades shall not prevail against it. <u>¹⁹ And I will give you the keys of the kingdom of heaven, and whatever you bind on earth will be bound in heaven, and whatever you loose on earth will be loosed in heaven."</u>

One of the keys to the kingdom is your answer to "Who do you say I am?" It also implies that the keys will be given later; probably after they received the Spirit.

When we say who Jesus is, He says who we are back to us and a fracture appears on our soul. When we forgive a fracture appears on our soul. When we extend mercy and grace toward others demonstrating the nature

The Ultimate Simulation

of God, fractures appear on our soul. Whenever we choose the ways of God over the way of flesh, fractures appear on our soul. We cannot yet be led by the Spirit, because our spirit has not been released. This is the work of Jesus, the logos, and the written Word of God. Merely reading the Word of God is not enough. We must believe it. How do you know if you believe it? You do it with no plan B.

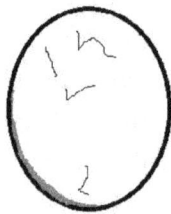

Fig. 5 An egg with cracks in its shell, symbolic of the soul.

If people say they are led by the Spirit and don't need to follow the Word or say they are covered by grace yet follow the way of flesh, there is no truth in them. Their soul has deceived them. If they say they have the New Testament and don't need the Old, they are either the product of bad teaching or deception. In either case, avoid them. If people say they are born again and it's been over a year since their rebirth and there is no difference in them, there is a problem.

At some point after repeated and frequent fractures, a small breech appears and we start to see who we are in relation to Jesus. Fortunately we don't get the full reality all at once or it would crush us. But God in His mercy gives us only as much as we can bear. A release comes when we truly <u>see</u> our fallen state and the glory of

The Ultimate Simulation

Jesus as our Savior, we fall on our face repenting and worshipping Him. At that point our soul is breeched enough for the release of the spirit, the blinders are lifted in those areas where the breech occurred and we begin to believe that Jesus is Lord. The work of Jesus as the destroyer of the works of the devil is at work and the work of the Spirit begins to the transformation of our hearts. However, the soul is not yet conquered and if left alone will do whatever it can to repair the breech and recapture the spirit. In like manner, the Spirit can only transform those areas where the soul covering has been broken.

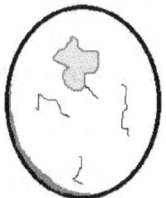

Fig. 6 An egg with cracks and a breech in its shell.

The heart is the way of flesh and until it is breeched (broken) and the spirit released, you are not a potential keeper. This is the beginning of the process of salvation. Think of it as a bird breaking out of its shell. Once the shell is broken, you start to breathe on your own and get a glimpse of another world outside the shell. The shell, the old man, tries to cling to you. All of us have issues, places where the shell isn't broken and clings to our soul. These are blind spots. These are present when we choose not to forgive, reject what the Word of God says, where curses haven't been broken, areas where the way of flesh is still the stronghold. The thing to remember

The Ultimate Simulation

is that we are not perfect. That won't happen until Jesus comes again. There is only one who is or will ever be sinless, Jesus. If we became spotless when we received Jesus, why would Paul say?

Philippians 2:12-13 ¹² Therefore, my beloved, as you have always obeyed, not as in my presence only, but now much more in my absence, work out your own salvation with fear and trembling; ¹³ for it is God who works in you both to will and to do for *His* good pleasure.

It is my opinion, we are never totally clean, otherwise there would be no need for mercy and grace. Mercy and grace are not forced upon us, but are available to us as part of the covenant. When Jesus tells the Laodiceans:

Revelation 3:15-16 ¹⁵ "I know your works, that you are neither cold nor hot. I could wish you were cold or hot. ¹⁶ So then, because you are lukewarm, and neither cold nor hot, I will vomit you out of My mouth.

What happened to mercy and grace for them? Lukewarm means they did nothing with their faith.

Matthew 7:21-23 ²¹ "Not everyone who says to Me, 'Lord, Lord,' shall enter the kingdom of heaven, but he who does the will of My Father in heaven. ²² Many will say to Me in that day, 'Lord, Lord, have we not prophesied in Your name, cast out demons in Your name, and done many wonders in Your name?' ²³ And then I will declare to them,

The Ultimate Simulation

'I never knew you; depart from Me, you who practice lawlessness!'

Some could argue that this means non-believers, but in Matt. 7 the keys are "in thy name done many wonderful works" and "I never knew you". Let me paraphrase, "Lord, we were good, we helped people, and we testified of you, people were blessed because of what we did in your name". This is the way of flesh. I believe I've heard it another way, "If just one person gets saved, it's worth it."

Now I'll say what the Lord hears, "I don't care what you told me to do, I did these good things to try and hide the fact I was disobedient. I buried the thing you gave me, because it didn't line up with my version of the truth or what I wanted to do. What you asked me to do would have been painful or embarrassing and I don't see how it could be in my best interest. I didn't want to spend the time to see what you wanted me to do; I didn't want others to know that I didn't talk with you, so I looked around and saw what you were doing in other places and started doing that. Isn't that just as good?"

When Jesus says "I never knew you"; it is in the same context as in Genesis, Adam knew Eve and she conceived. My version of what Jesus said, **"I gave you seed and you aborted it. You never brought forth the fruit I asked you to produce. You treated my intimacy with distain. What you perceive as fruit never justifies disobedience. You don't know me nor me you."**

The Ultimate Simulation

Can you not see that disobedience is the way of flesh? It's not what you do that makes you His, it's what you do with the seed He plants in you, the "revealed" word given just to you. Is this not the same as the parables about the talents and the sower?

> **Revelation: To use the name of the Lord without knowing Him or to use His name without faith is sin, because you are taking the name of the Lord in vain.**
> **(3rd commandment)**

He has not called us to be sinless; He's called us to be faithful. Here's where most of us miss it. We try to be holy through religion.

This is the way of the flesh. Trying to be something we're not. Too many people exist for Jesus and very few 'live' for Him. Life is not a burden, it is to be savored and enjoyed. How can you say "The joy of the Lord is my strength" when out of your mouth comes defeat, denial and despair? You're a victim of circumstances instead of a circumstance over comer. You drink the Kool-Aid of the world and want God to rescue you out of this evil place. Do others want what you radiate? If not, you're not 'living' for Him and are not His. The release of the spirit is the completion of the restorative work of Jesus. Then begins the work of the Holy Spirit; working with your spirit to transform your mind.

At this point, JESUS HAS DONE ALL HE WILL DO FOR YOU, HIS WORK IS FINISHED, the rest is up to you.

The Ultimate Simulation

Without your mind completing the transformation process, you cannot enter into the kingdom.

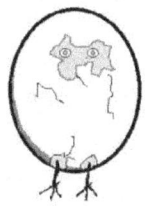

Fig. 7 An egg with eyes and feet exposed.

You cannot see the kingdom of God, until the release of the spirit occurs and you are born again.

John 3:3 ³ Jesus answered and said to him, "Most assuredly, I say to you, unless one is born again, he cannot see the kingdom of God."

Another diversion.

1 Corinthians 13:13 ¹³ And now abideth faith, hope, love, these three; but the greatest of these *is* love.

So here in the summary verse of the "love" chapter, everything is put in perspective with charity being the Greek word agape (the God kind of love). This represents a process. You cannot enter into love without hope and you cannot enter into hope without faith and you cannot enter into faith without hearing and you cannot hear without seeking and learning to recognize that still small voice.

John 10:1-4 ¹ "Most assuredly, I say to you, he who does not enter the sheepfold by the door, but climbs up some other way, the same is a thief and a robber. ² But he who enters by the door is the shepherd of the sheep. ³ To him the doorkeeper opens, and the sheep hear his voice; and he calls his own sheep by name and leads them out. ⁴ And when he brings out his own sheep, he goes before them; <u>and the sheep follow him, for they know his voice.</u> ⁵ <u>Yet they will by no means follow a stranger, but will flee from him, for they do not know the voice of strangers.</u>"

If you don't know His voice, I suggest you set aside quiet time for seeking Him on a regular basis. Ask to hear His voice and keep a log of impressions, dreams and answered prayer. It may take a while, but it is my experience that persistence pays off. Otherwise you'll never breech your shell and live a defeated life trying to be religious.

Romans 10:17 ¹⁷ So then <u>faith *comes* by hearing, and hearing by the word of God.</u>

Of the two Greek words for "word", logos and rhema, this one is rhema. While both apply to God's word, I believe rhema is what God says to me in an "aha" moment. A moment when hearing or reading the logos word, it is accompanied with revelation. There can be a lot of argument over this point, but everything with God is relationship based. Just reading the Word does not bring faith. Reading the Word with the anticipation of the God of everything communicating with you, sets the stage for rhema. To paraphrase, faith comes by me personally receiving revelation through the Word of God and I activate faith by being obedient and doing it. The rhema word can never be in opposition to the logos word. Also, contained within the rhema word is supernatural power sufficient to accomplish what was said.

The work of the Spirit is to reveal the things of God and guide you in truth. If you claim to have the 'truth' then you are not teachable, because you already know everything you need to be saved. This also is the way of flesh, because it's only concerned about your salvation. Yet your very attitude denies your salvation.

Jesus never preached the church or salvation, He preached the Kingdom. Salvation is something that happens as a result of entering into the kingdom by faith, not as a door to the kingdom.

For more on the soul and spirit read "Release of the Spirit" by Watchman Nee.

The second response of Jesus was:

John 3:5-6 [5] Jesus answered, Verily, verily, I say unto thee, <u>Except a man be born of water and *of* the Spirit, he cannot enter into the kingdom of God</u>. [6] That which is born of the flesh is flesh; and that which is born of the Spirit is spirit.

The water is the washing of the water of the word (Jesus, logos, restoration). The washing away of your sins through the shedding of His blood and the work of the cross. This is the place where 99% of the church stops. They are in effect Old Testament Christians. It's all about what Jesus did. To move on requires you to take responsibility for your own actions. You must leave behind the 'milk' of the word and move into the 'meat'. Meat is

The Ultimate Simulation

only for the mature. The truth is that at this point you have only pierced the outer veil and moved from the outer court into the inner court. That is all the farther Jesus can take you. The kingdom is the holy of holies and cannot be seen from the outer court. It can only be seen from the inner court.

There is a second rebirth into the kingdom which can only happen by way of activation of the spirit to Spirit link whereby the Son and the Father dwell in you by way of the Spirit. This activation was not in the 1st Adam and the very angels are anxious to see what its' all about. To be born of the Spirit is to be linked with Him in a cohabitation of your mind. This can only happen through the work of transformation by the Spirit.

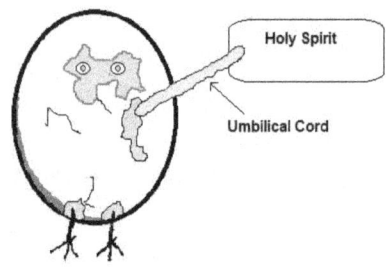

Fig. 8 An egg with its spirit released and linked to the Holy Spirit.

1 Peter 1:6-12 ⁶ In this you greatly rejoice, though now for a little while, if need be, you have been grieved by various trials, ⁷ that the genuineness of your faith, *being* much more precious than gold that perishes, though it is tested by fire, may be found to praise, honor, and glory at

The Ultimate Simulation

the revelation of Jesus Christ, [8] whom having not seen you love. Though now you do not see *Him,* yet believing, you rejoice with joy inexpressible and full of glory, [9] receiving the end of your faith—the salvation of *your* souls.

[10] Of this salvation the prophets have inquired and searched carefully, who prophesied of the grace *that would come* to you, [11] searching what, or what manner of time, the Spirit of Christ who was in them was indicating when He testified beforehand the sufferings of Christ and the glories that would follow. [12] To them it was revealed that, not to themselves, but to us they were ministering the things which now have been reported to you through those who have preached the gospel to you by the Holy Spirit sent from heaven—things which angels desire to look into.

I think Romans 8 is to be read in the light of the process just discussed.

Roman 8:1-20 [1] T*here is* therefore now no condemnation to those who are in Christ Jesus, who do not walk according to the flesh, but according to the Spirit. [2] For the law of the Spirit of life in Christ Jesus has made me free from the law of sin and death. [3] For what the law could not do in that it was weak through the flesh, God *did* by sending His own Son in the likeness of sinful flesh, on account of sin: He condemned sin in the flesh, [4] that the righteous requirement of the law might be fulfilled in us who do not walk according to the flesh but according to the Spirit. [5] For those who live according to the flesh set their minds on the things of the flesh, but those *who live* according to the Spirit, the things of the Spirit. [6] For to be carnally minded *is* death, but to be spiritually minded *is* life and peace. [7] Because the carnal mind *is* enmity against

The Ultimate Simulation

God; for it is not subject to the law of God, nor indeed can be. [8] So then, those who are in the flesh cannot please God.

[9] But you are not in the flesh but in the Spirit, if indeed the Spirit of God dwells in you. Now if anyone does not have the Spirit of Christ, he is not His. [10] And if Christ *is* in you, the body *is* dead because of sin, but the Spirit *is* life because of righteousness. [11] But if the Spirit of Him who raised Jesus from the dead dwells in you, He who raised Christ from the dead will also give life to your mortal bodies through His Spirit who dwells in you.

[12] Therefore, brethren, we are debtors—not to the flesh, to live according to the flesh. [13] For if you live according to the flesh you will die; but if by the Spirit you put to death the deeds of the body, you will live. [14] For as many as are led by the Spirit of God, these are sons of God. [15] For you did not receive the spirit of bondage again to fear, but you received the Spirit of adoption by whom we cry out, "Abba, Father." [16] The Spirit Himself bears witness with our spirit that we are children of God, [17] and if children, then heirs—heirs of God and joint heirs with Christ, if indeed we suffer with *Him,* that we may also be glorified together.

[18] For I consider that the sufferings of this present time are not worthy *to be compared* with the glory which shall be revealed in us. [19] For the earnest expectation of the creation eagerly waits for the revealing of the sons of God. [20] For the creation was subjected to futility, not willingly, but because of Him who subjected *it* in hope; [21] because the creation itself also will be delivered from the bondage of corruption into the glorious liberty of the children of God.

The Ultimate Simulation

Only sons can enter into the kingdom. Only the Spirit can pierce the inner veil, whereby we can live and not die in the presence of the Almighty.

After His baptism, Jesus was led by the Spirit into the desert. This is analogous to the walk that the Spirit has for us. It is always painful, but extraordinarily fruitful. However, this is not the test. The test comes after the walk when we are required to stand on our own. We live or die by what is inside us. Notice in the testing of Jesus, He quotes what God has said. During a test, you cannot bring sources or reference material with you. During a test, God withdraws to see what is inside of you and what comes out during the pressing. Each test is individual and according to what He has called you to do. It is during this testing in the desert that God requires you to travail and birth the seed(s) implanted in you by the Spirit. (It kind of sounds like Revelation). Power flows from birthing. I like Luke's account of this because in the first two temptations Jesus quotes the word (logos) "It is written...." Then the devil quotes logos back to Him "It is written..." where Jesus replies with rhema "It is said..." The devil will fight against the logos word, but gives up when it's apparent that the rhema word is fully functioning.

Luke 4:1-14 ¹ Then Jesus, being filled with the Holy Spirit, returned from the Jordan and was led by the Spirit into the wilderness, ² being tempted for forty days by the devil. And in those days He ate nothing, and afterward, when they had ended, He was hungry. ³ And the devil said to Him, "If You are the Son of God, command this stone to become bread."

The Ultimate Simulation

⁴ But Jesus answered him, saying, "It is written, '*Man shall not live by bread alone,* but by every word of God.' "

⁵ Then the devil, taking Him up on a high mountain, showed Him all the kingdoms of the world in a moment of time. ⁶ And the devil said to Him, "All this authority I will give You, and their glory; for *this* has been delivered to me, and I give it to whomever I wish. ⁷ Therefore, if You will worship before me, all will be Yours."

⁸ And Jesus answered and said to him, "Get behind Me, Satan! For it is written, '*You shall worship the* LORD *your God, and Him only you shall serve.*' "

⁹ Then he brought Him to Jerusalem, set Him on the pinnacle of the temple, and said to Him, "If You are the Son of God, throw Yourself down from here. ¹⁰ For it is written:

'He shall give His angels charge over you, *To keep you,*' ¹¹ and, 'In their *hands they shall bear you up,* Lest you dash your foot against a stone.' "

¹² And Jesus answered and said to him, "It has been said, '*You shall not* tempt the LORD your God.' "

¹³ Now when the devil had ended every temptation, he departed from Him until an opportune time. ¹⁴ Then Jesus returned in the power of the Spirit to Galilee, and news of Him went out through all the surrounding region.

So Jesus went into the wilderness full of the Holy Spirit, but came out in the power of the Spirit. Being full of the Spirit didn't automatically position Him into the

The Ultimate Simulation

kingdom, but was the beginning of a process whereby Jesus gave birth to His destiny and emerged in power.

To see the kingdom <u>we must be born again</u> of the Word, to enter the kingdom <u>we must birth</u> what the Spirit impregnates us with. When the Spirit says to us to go to an enemy and repent or simply to tell someone who has hurt us that we love them and forgive, how is that different than Michael coming to Mary saying she is about to give birth? The seed wasn't placed in Mary by Jesus, it was by the Spirit. Are we not birthing the things of God? It is only when we birth what He has given us, that we enter the kingdom. We continue in the kingdom through continued obedience, humility, producing fruit and planting new seeds.

A phenomenal thing happens when we give birth to the seed of the Spirit; the part of our mind that was submitted to the will of the Father is transformed. It is at that time the Spirit replaces our desires with the desires of the Father and our mind is renewed. This is not a one-time thing, because just like the shell, the mind tries to return to its unrenewed state and without continually submitting it will forget about what the Spirit has done. The enemy will not stop sowing seeds of doubt.

The Ultimate Simulation

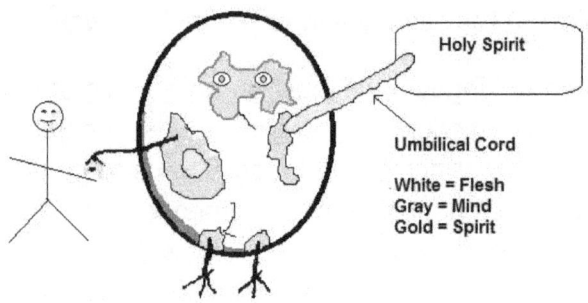

Fig. 8 An egg feeding others with Spirit.

Rev. 22:12 ¹² And, behold, I come quickly; and my reward *is* with me, to give every man according as his work shall be.

Let me make this clear "to give everyone according to what he has done with the seed(s) given by the Spirit". The parable of the talents applies here.

The seeds are your responsibility to tend to. Your work is not to be kind, loving and turn the other cheek. These come as the result of a transformed mind. Your work is to plant the seeds and do what is necessary for them to bear fruit.

Let's continue with John 3

John 3:6-8 ⁶ That which is born of the flesh is flesh; and that which is born of the Spirit is spirit. ⁷ Marvel not that I said unto thee, Ye must be born again. ⁸ The wind bloweth where it listeth, and thou hearest the sound thereof, but canst not tell whence it cometh, and whither it goeth: so is every one that is born of the Spirit.

The Ultimate Simulation

This is at the heart of everything said up to this point and verse eight is the summary of it all. To understand verse eight, I will use Tom's inverse rule, which states that "If a thing is true, its inverse is also true".

Using this tool, the inverse of verse 8 is, "If you are not born of the Spirit, your past, present and future are completely predictable", (fatalism). So by being born of the Spirit we can transcend the laws of the universe and its predictability. This is free will, whereby anything not of self and not in opposition to the Word of God is possible. I have submitted my will to the will of the Father by being led by the Spirit through the desert testings and in travail give birth to the things of God which override the laws of fatalism and flesh. This is what it means to enter into the kingdom and do the deeds of Jesus. It is only after we enter the kingdom we can say to the mountain 'move' and have it obey us. This is NOT a onetime decision. At no time does God ever take control. This is a moment by moment process. The further I go, the easier the decisions get because His faithfulness and love towards me are amplified with each new step of obedience.

Revelation: After prolonged faithfulness, through persecutions and revelations, belief turns into knowing.

As you mature in areas of your life, you take more responsibility for your decisions. A number of years ago I was talking to the Spirit about an issue and He said ***"Don't you know me by now? You're a big boy. So***

The Ultimate Simulation

do what you know to do." It hit me like an arrow in the heart, but He was right. He was weaning me away from the milk. Rather severely, if I might say. If you are still praying about everything, then you are still a babe! Grow up and be responsible and accountable for your decisions and actions. Only those who don't know Him as friend or lover require help with everything. He won't always be your babysitter. As you mature His leadership methods change. He never leaves you, but requires more of you. If it's ever easy then it probably isn't God.

The way we are made, we only learn by pain. We can accept something as true, but we only learn it when its associated pain is experienced. If we experience things without pain, then we think there are no consequences associated with it. Love doesn't deter you from doing something that may be against God's will, but fear will. You worship what you fear, not what you love. If you do not fear God then you cannot love Him. Without the fear of God, you have no appreciation for mercy and grace. Without the fear of God you are not wise, but foolish. Without the fear of God there is nothing to save. 1st comes the law which establishes the fear of God and consequences. Without the fear of God you will leave Him at the slightest hint of pain. The "wouldn't hurt a flea Jesus", is a figment of your imagination and is used to justify your liberal ideas about a "there, there" God. Jesus wasn't a nice man. It was His way or the highway. Would a nice man lash people with a whip? Would a nice man call others vipers and empty tombs? Would a nice man curse a fig tree? Would a nice man give people hard sayings that

The Ultimate Simulation

crushed them? Would a nice man call a foreign woman a dog? What would today's media do with that? However, He did have compassion on the disadvantaged. He only displayed mercy and grace where mercy and grace were warranted. Jesus was anything but politically correct. Pain overcomes logic and pain overcomes emotions. If the Lord chastises those He loves, your "no pain" Jesus can't save you because he is, in your mind, a psychological construct.

Chapter 7: Players

To me this part of the simulation is about who gets to go on to the next phase. I choose to call them "keepers". Since the Bible is the story of the sons of God, then human beings are not the top of the food chain. It can be argued that humans are animals that appear to be sentient. Adam and Eve were two of the human animals God chose to breathe into them the breath of life. Animals exist; they don't live in the context of God's purposes. Are there other animals that have been given this opportunity? While I don't have direct scripture, it can be implied from:

John 14:2 [2] In My Father's house are many mansions; if *it were* not *so,* would have told you. I go to prepare a place for you.

Does the reference to rooms or mansions refer only to this creation and possibly other species or could it refer to other creations? In a simulation it is easy to start another instance with the same or different parameters.

Also it is my opinion that the living creatures before the throne that have four different faces, cherub, man, lion and eagle, are the creatures in this sub simulation that have been given the breath of life. That is why they are called 'living creatures'. Is it coincidental that in many ancient cultures gods are depicted as beings with these same heads?

Ezekiel 10:14 [14] Each one had four faces: the first face *was* the face of a cherub, the second face the face of a man,

The Ultimate Simulation

the third the face of a lion, and the fourth the face of an eagle.

In this part of the simulation, the top of the chain of potential sons are human beings who have at sometime accepted Jesus. As such, I classify them into the following categories.

1. **Former Players** – These are those who accepted Jesus and the Holy Spirit. Had tasted of the power of the Holy Spirit and then rejected Him. No amount of prayer can save them.

Hebrews 6:4-6 [4] For *it is* impossible for those who were once enlightened, and have tasted the heavenly gift, and have become partakers of the Holy Spirit, [5] and have tasted the good word of God and the powers of the age to come, [6] if they fall away, to renew them again to repentance, since they crucify again for themselves the Son of God, and put *Him* to an open shame.

2. **Reprobate Minds** – These are people who at one time knew Jesus then gave themselves over to hedonism (pursuit of the flesh and doctrines of demons). For all practical purposes they have no potential of ever fulfilling what God has for them. I will not say it is impossible, but it would take massive amounts of prayer and intercession to have the potential to change their destination.

Romans 1:28-32 [28] And even as they did not like to retain God in *their* knowledge, God gave them over to a reprobate mind, to do those things which are not convenient; [29] Being filled with all unrighteousness,

The Ultimate Simulation

fornication, wickedness, covetousness, maliciousness; full of envy, murder, debate, deceit, malignity; whisperers, [30] Backbiters, haters of God, despiteful, proud, boasters, inventors of evil things, disobedient to parents, [31] Without understanding, covenant breakers, without natural affection, implacable, unmerciful: [32] <u>Who knowing the judgment of God, that they which commit such things are worthy of death, not only do the same, but have pleasure in them that do them.</u>

3. **Vortex Minds** – These are those who are caught in the vortex of persistent sin. However, there is still a possibility for them to repent.

Genesis 15:16 [16] But in the fourth generation they shall return here, for the iniquity of the Amorites *is* not yet complete."

Romans 6:23 [23] For the wages of sin *is* death, but the gift of God *is* eternal life in Christ Jesus our Lord.

Mark 4:11-12 [11] And He said to them, "To you it has been given to know the mystery of the kingdom of God; but to those who are outside, all things come in parables, [12] so that '<u>Seeing they may see and not perceive, *And hearing they may hear and not understand;*</u> Lest they should turn, And their *sins be forgiven them.*'"

4. **Lazy Minds** – These are those who do nothing but the bare minimum. Outer darkness is their future. In my opinion, those in outer darkness have done enough to avoid the lake of fire, but miss the spirit of what is required. They are left with the knowledge of what could

have been. Some argue that these try and take possession of a soul to try and gain a second chance which can never work. Possible?

Matthew 25:26-30 [26] "But his lord answered and said to him, 'You wicked and lazy servant, you knew that I reap where I have not sown, and gather where I have not scattered seed. [27] So you ought to have deposited my money with the bankers, and at my coming I would have received back my own with interest. [28] So take the talent from him, and give *it* to him who has ten talents.

[29] 'For to everyone who has, more will be given, and he will have abundance; but from him who does not have, even what he has will be taken away. [30] And cast the unprofitable servant into the outer darkness. There will be weeping and gnashing of teeth.'

James 2:26 [26] For as the body without the spirit is dead, so faith without works is dead also.

    5.   **Partial Minds** – These are those who only accept the part of the word they like and assume no responsibility for the whole word. Their lot is also outer darkness.

Matthew 7:21-23 [21] "Not everyone who says to Me, 'Lord, Lord,' shall enter the kingdom of heaven, but he who does the will of My Father in heaven. [22] Many will say to Me in that day, 'Lord, Lord, have we not prophesied in Your name, cast out demons in Your name, and done many wonders in Your name?' [23] And then I will declare to them, 'I never knew you; depart from Me, you who practice lawlessness!'

The Ultimate Simulation

Matthew 22:11-13 [11] "But when the king came in to see the guests, he saw a man there who did not have on a wedding garment. [12] So he said to him, 'Friend, how did you come in here without a wedding garment?' And he was speechless. [13] Then the king said to the servants, 'Bind him hand and foot, take him away, and cast *him* into outer darkness; there will be weeping and gnashing of teeth.'

      6.   **Babes** – Greek Nepios - Those new in the Lord and or who have never progressed beyond Jesus is Savior.

1 Peter 2:1-3 [1] Therefore, laying aside all malice, all deceit, hypocrisy, envy, and all evil speaking, [2] as newborn babes, desire the pure milk of the word, that you may grow thereby, [3] if indeed you have tasted that the Lord *is* gracious.

      7.   **Children** – Greek Paidion - Jesus is Lord

      8.   **Teenagers** – Greek Teknon - Jesus is King

      9.   **Sons** – Greek Huios - Jesus is Friend – being led by the Holy Spirit

      10.   **Fathers** – Greek Pater - Jesus is Lover – living in the Holy Spirit

There is another Greek word, *Telios* – One flesh with God or complete. (I believe it will only happen after Jesus returns and will apply to all keepers).

For more information on the levels of relationship, please read *The Link* by Tom Long.

The Ultimate Simulation

For the most part, only the last five are keepers. Of the five, sons (kings) will rule and fathers (priests) will reign. The others will be part of the host of heaven.

Becoming a keeper is a process, not an event. Although, it starts with the event of repentance and asking the Lord into your heart.

Philippians 2:12-16 [12] Therefore, my beloved, as you have always obeyed, not as in my presence only, but now much more in my absence, <u>work out your own salvation with fear and trembling;</u> [13] for it is God who works in you both to will and to do for *His* good pleasure. [14] Do all things without complaining and disputing, [15] <u>that you may become blameless and harmless, children of God</u> without fault in the midst of a crooked and perverse generation, among whom you shine as lights in the world, [16] holding fast the word of life, so that I may rejoice in the day of Christ that I have not run in vain or labored in vain.

> **Revelation: Jesus is the door to restoration and the Holy Spirit is the door to transformation.**

Romans 12:2 [2] <u>And do not be conformed to this world, but be transformed by the renewing of your mind,</u> that you may prove what *is* that good and acceptable and perfect will of God.

Romans 8:14 [14] <u>For as many as are led by the Spirit of God, these are sons of God.</u>

The Ultimate Simulation

Without "keepers" I see no purpose to the simulation.

Chapter 8: The Multiverse

Genesis 1:1 [1] In the beginning, God created the heavens and the earth.

2 Corinthians 12:2 [2] I know a man in Christ who fourteen years ago was caught up to the third heaven—whether in the body or out of the body I do not know, God knows.

We know from scripture there are at least three heavens. There are at least three alternate realities, Sheol and Abaddon below and Paradise above.

Proverbs 15:11 [11] Sheol and Abaddon lie open before the Lord; how much more the hearts of the children of man!

Luke 23:43 [43] And he said to him, "Truly, I say to you, today you will be with me in paradise."

There seems to be a set of different dimensions for souls or are they a reference to lower and upper heavens?

Revelation 21:1 [1] Then I saw a new heaven and a new earth, for the first heaven and the first earth had passed away, and the sea was no more.

Sounds like the reality bubble of the first heaven collapsed. Question is, are we being moved to a new reality bubble or are we outside the black hole that contained our old bubble?

The Ultimate Simulation

Psalms 113:4-6 ⁴ The Lord is high above all nations, and his glory above the heavens! ⁵ Who is like the Lord our God, who is seated on high, ⁶ who looks far down on the heavens and the earth?

Ephesians 4:10 ¹⁰ He who descended is the one who also ascended far above all the heavens, that he might fill all things.

In a simulation, what is above the simulation is the operating system and the control program or AI.

Are there multiple simulations running under the same control program? If so, could there be incidental intersection points or portals?

Genesis 28:10-12 ¹⁰ Now Jacob went out from Beersheba and went toward Haran. ¹¹ So he came to a certain place and stayed there all night, because the sun had set. And he took one of the stones of that place and put it at his head, and he lay down in that place to sleep. ¹² Then he dreamed, and behold, a ladder *was* set up on the earth, and its top reached to heaven; and there the angels of God were ascending and descending on it.

John 1:51 ⁵¹ And He said to him, "Most assuredly, I say to you, hereafter you shall see heaven open, and the angels of God ascending and descending upon the Son of Man."

If this simulation isn't version 1, then it can't be the only one.

Is the AI self learning in that the successful runs allow the local simulation architect to be merged with the controlling AI?

The Ultimate Simulation

In a simulation, everything is made up of something, except for the programming. There is no "spooky spiritual" stuff.

Revelation 20:1-3 [1] Then I saw an angel coming down from heaven, holding in his hand the key to the bottomless pit and a great chain. [2] And he seized the dragon, that ancient serpent, who is the devil and Satan, and bound him for a thousand years, [3] and <u>threw him into the pit, and shut it and sealed it over him,</u> so that he might not deceive the nations any longer, until the thousand years were ended. After that he must be released for a little while.

If angels are spirit beings, how can they be held in a bottomless pit (akin to a portal to a black hole or another dimension) unless their spirit is made up of something that can be contained? There may be object properties that are reserved only for the control programs and their agents.

Chapter 9: Dimensions and Portals

I believe the number of Jesus is 13. (Twelve disciples plus one). I believe it is hated by superstitionists for that very reason.

John 1:1-3 ¹ In the beginning was the Word, and the Word was with God, and the Word was God. ² He was in the beginning with God. ³ All things were made through him, and without him was not anything made that was made.

Since all things were made by him, his number should be one of the cornerstones of creation.

I believe there are 13 dimensions, although I don't have a direct word or revelation.

One day as I was reading Matthew 17, the question came **"Who appeared on the mountain and what did they have in common?"**

Matthew 17:1-3 ¹ Now after six days Jesus took Peter, James, and John his brother, led them up on a high mountain by themselves; ² and He was transfigured before them. His face shone like the sun, and His clothes became as white as the light. ³ And behold, Moses and Elijah appeared to them, talking with Him.

Moses and Elijah were both in a cave on Mt. Sinai, at different times of course. Both had an experience with the Lord. Both needed encouragement. It appears both time traveled into the presence of Jesus. How did the

The Ultimate Simulation

disciples know it was Moses and Elijah? Is there a portal on Mt. Sinai?

John 8:56 ⁵⁶ Your father Abraham rejoiced to see My day, and he saw *it* and was glad."

      Did Abraham also time travel or was this in a vision?

      Some believe the Ark of the Covenant was a portal generator. Possible?

Chapter 10: A Primary Field

If all creation glorifies Him, then it seems to reason that the way He describes Himself would tell us how this creation is made.

Romans 1:20 [20] For since the creation of the world His invisible *attributes* are clearly seen, being understood by the things that are made, *even* His eternal power and Godhead

Deuteronomy 6:4 [4] "Hear, O Israel: The LORD our God, the LORD is one.

1Corinthians 12:4-6 [4] Now there are varieties of gifts, but the same Spirit; [5] and there are varieties of service, but the same Lord; [6] and there are varieties of activities, but it is the same God who empowers them all in everyone.

Matthew 24:36 [36] "But concerning that day and hour no one knows, not even the angels of heaven, nor the Son, but the Father only.

The basis for Christianity is one God in three persons. (Father, Son and Holy Spirit).

To summarize:

1. Father is in charge of purpose and time
2. Son is in charge of matter and how it responds to authority.
3. Holy Spirit is in charge of supernatural power and drawing people to the Father.

The Ultimate Simulation

Scripture usually categorizes them as the will of the Father, the mind of Christ and the power of the Holy Spirit.

So I conclude there is one primary field with three states that is the basis of this simulation. It is possible this field is triangular in shape. While positive or negative charges have different identities. Is it possible gravity is the sum of zero state charges overlays.

Isn't it coincidental, the similarity of this and loop quantum gravity?

I can't imagine any particular reason that God would describe Himself as triune except if it is a key to understanding this creation.

This is also repeated in the control program with three sections.

Father AI oversees the time/space matrix and forecasts the future to insure the goals are met. He is the keeper of the rules and quantum laws.

The Son AI oversees the architecture and management of the simulation to optimize the Fathers goals and is keeper of physical laws.

The Spirit AI oversees supernatural power distributions to optimize the Fathers goals by drawing keepers and empowering possibilities and keeper of wave laws.

The Ultimate Simulation

John 1:18 [18]No one has seen God at any time. The only begotten Son, who is in the bosom of the Father, He has declared *Him*.

In a simulation, no one ever sees the control program.

The simulation was designed to produce AI that emulated the characteristics as set forth in the rules. Jesus was the first born who became the Christ after His design and management of this simulation. Then took His position in the Son AI to which in the future other Sons will be added.

Space is made up of these fields as a matrix. These could not be a memory cell matrix because that would denote an absolute location. They are kept in a quasi-stable condition by what I'll call micromagnetism. Like a board full of magnets seeks stability unless an outside force is introduced. Think of space/time, matter and supernatural power as spreadsheets each with its own rules.

While matter is its own spreadsheet, it interacts with the time/space spreadsheet via the six energies as described earlier.

Time, space and matter are completely fatalistic, being controlled by the rules of the simulation, their individual spreadsheet rules, and the energy rules that control their interaction.

The Ultimate Simulation

The states of these primary fields are +1, 0, and 1. The more fields overlay, the greater the charge.

The third spreadsheet is the Holy Spirit, who adds unpredictability to the equation.

1 Corinthians 12:11 [11] But one and the same Spirit works all these things, distributing to each one individually as He wills.

Romans 8:14 [14] For as many as are led by the Spirit of God, these are sons of God.

The Bible is not the story of homo-sapiens, it is the story of the sons of God.

Everything is preparing us to be creators and managers of our own sub-simulation. But we have to develop our talents to go outside the fatalistic box in search of fulfilling the prime directive of making creative sons.

Everything is centered on possibilities in pursuit of Him. At the point in time we have no possibilities, we are no different than animals which cannot act outside the program. This simulation isn't about being saved; it's about being declared keepers with possibilities.

All who have possibilities are given a measure of faith.

Romans 12:3 [3] For I say, through the grace given to me, to everyone who is among you, not to think *of himself* more

The Ultimate Simulation

highly than he ought to think, but to think soberly, <u>as God has dealt to each one a measure of faith.</u>

The context of the above scripture is only to believers.

Hebrews 11:1 [1] <u>Now faith is the substance of things hoped for, the evidence of things not seen.</u>

Hebrews 11:6 [6] <u>But without faith *it is* impossible to please *Him*,</u> for he who comes to God must believe that He is, and *that* He is a rewarder of those who diligently seek Him.

Romans 10:17 [17] So then <u>faith *comes* by hearing, and hearing by the word of God.</u>

By faith we come into agreement with what God has said and is saying through His Holy Spirit which causes us to resonate like a tuning fork with the third spreadsheet and power can flow to alter reality.

The limits of our ability to alter reality is directly related to and limited to our authority (dominion) and to the extent we agree with it. There are limits, for example we do not have authority over Satan, anything outside our dimension or God's end-game.

Faith and the God kind of love are spelled RISK. Going beyond what our senses tell us and transforming our minds to becoming creative sons.

To overcome the potential failures, God offers mercy and grace to those who try.

The Ultimate Simulation

Luke 15:4-7 ⁴"What man of you, having a hundred sheep, if he loses one of them, does not leave the ninety-nine in the wilderness, <u>and go after the one which is lost until he finds it</u>? ⁵ And when he has found *it,* he lays *it* on his shoulders, rejoicing. ⁶ And when he comes home, he calls together *his* friends and neighbors, saying to them, 'Rejoice with me, for I have found my sheep which was lost!' ⁷ I say to you that likewise there will be more joy in heaven over one sinner who repents than over ninety-nine just persons who need no repentance.

I see this as the one who is willing to stretch the boundaries and extend the possibilities. They are the ones the Lord goes after. Here's one with possibilities. It doesn't matter if we make mistakes; it's that we have possibilities for the kingdom. With those that play it safe, herd mentality, there are no possibilities and consequently no faith. To the extent that we can overcome the desires of the flesh (fatalism or God made me this way), we become keepers. As long as we justify our disobedience to what God says, our ability to be led by the Spirit diminishes until it is fulfilled that the wages of persistent sin is death.

Romans 6:23 ²³ <u>For the wages of sin *is* death</u>, but the gift of God *is* eternal life in Christ Jesus our Lord.

Chapter 11: Quantum Entanglement

Simply put, quantum entanglement is the linking of two or more particles in such a way that when the state of one is measured the others also reflect the same state no matter how far apart they are.

In a simulation, every object has a location reference. What if the reference property isn't an item, but a list? Albeit, 99.99999% are unary. The list isn't resolved until it needs to be rendered. If this is the case, it should be possible to have more than two particles entangled. Also, if entanglement is at the particle level, it should also be at the field level and it should be possible at ever increasing object sizes. (Atom, molecule, a complete object). If I could analyze an object and then entangle each particle with a corresponding particle, then I could teleport anything, especially in a simulation where soul and spirit are quantifiable.

Maybe, it's simpler and I only need to entangle the object location reference, because the internal references will resolve themselves when rendered.

In a contained object the field location is probably relative to the containing object. If the transported object were destroyed, it should be possible to reconstitute the original although it would be without any memory of what happened after the transport.

I know this is programmer speak. Sorry.

Chapter 12: A Hologram

John 8:12 [12] Then Jesus spoke to them again, saying, "<u>I am the light of the world</u>. He who follows Me shall not walk in darkness, but have the light of life."

John 1:3 [3] <u>All things were made through Him, and without Him nothing was made that was made.</u>

Since Jesus refers to Himself as light and all things were made by him, it's not too far a leap to propose we are living in a hologram. At least consider it a possibility.

In this simulation, I believe there is a possibility the time/space matrix and objects are made of light emitted from a holographic projector in each dimension.

Revelation 22:1 [1] And he showed <u>me a pure river of water of life, clear as crystal, proceeding from the throne of God and of the Lamb.</u>

Is the throne of God a holographic projector and the waters of life are light waves?

Is the description of the throne, elders and living creatures dimension or reality bubble specific?

Possibilities.

You may be wondering how long it would take to display this hologram. In a simulation, time is controlled by a centralized clock. In essence, everything is updated with each tick of the clock. If it takes 1000 years of time to

The Ultimate Simulation

produce 1 day of simulation time, objects within the simulation wouldn't know. It would be seamless to them.

2 Peter 3:8 ⁸ But, beloved, do not forget this one thing, that <u>with the Lord one day *is* as a thousand years, and a thousand years as one day</u>.

Chapter 13: Black Holes

Black holes are stellar objects that have such intense gravity that not even light can escape. They appear to be at the center of every galaxy, but can be anywhere where certain kinds of stars die and collapse into an extremely dense core. Any object getting too close will be pulled in and pulled apart due to the extreme forces.

Genesis 1:1:3 [1] In the beginning, God created the heavens and the earth. [2] <u>The earth was without form and void</u>, and darkness was over the face of the deep. And the Spirit of God was hovering over the face of the waters. [3] And God said, "Let there be light," and there was light.

As I have said before, there is nothing written that says what follows verse 1 is a description of verse 1. What if the heavens and earth were created in verse 1 and then Earth and a lot of other matter were captured by a black hole. The word "was" can also be translated "became". Doesn't "the earth became without form and void" describe what would happen if it were captured by a black hole?

2 Peter 3:10 [10] But the day of the Lord will come as a thief in the night, in which <u>the heavens will pass away with a great noise, and the elements will melt with fervent heat; both the earth and the works that are in it will be burned up.</u>

Since both the heavens and earth will be melted, it sure sounds like the collapse of the reality bubble.

The Ultimate Simulation

A couple of years ago, I was just minding my own business when out of the blue comes **"Black holes are farms."**

As a result of this Word I concluded back holes then are creative engines used to explore possibilities. As each one ruptures, a new set of possibilities is set into motion with its own big bang. Each rupture and subsequent collapse represents a genesis cycle. Untold billions of black holes in the known universe could mean there are seemingly endless possibilities. If this is true, what a marvelous mind put this together.

What possible force could cause the black hole to rupture?

The Holy Spirit is the force that adds power to whatever agrees with the prime laws, statutes, precepts,... and purpose that already have been declared.

So the Holy Spirit is hovering over this plasma soup waiting for a declaration of faith. And when God or one of His agents by faith said, "Let there be light", the plasma all vibrate in unity and with the power of the Holy Spirit cause a breach.

In Genesis 1, the Hebrew word for God, Elohiym, is plural in form. That is why God says "Let us..." While most theologians believe this refers to the Trinity, there are other possibilities.

The Ultimate Simulation

Hebrews 11:3 ³ By faith we understand that the worlds were framed by the word of God, so that the things which are seen were not made of things which are visible.

The voice of God is really when either God or His agent speaks then everything at the bottom of a black hole comes into synchronous vibration that over powers gravity causing a breach by the creation of a singularity probably with a big bang. This breach could push a reality bubble out in a new dimension.

In the Bible things happen only when God speaks. So I believe there is a specific frequency for this voice. I believe that is the resonant frequency of the basic field that makes up everything. When all creation comes into unity anything within the rules of the simulation are possible.

Genesis 1:1:5 ¹ In the beginning, God created the heavens and the earth. ² The earth was without form and void, and darkness was over the face of the deep. <u>And the Spirit of God was hovering over the face of the waters.</u> ³ And God said, "Let there be light," and there was light. ⁴ And God saw that the light was good. And God separated the light from the darkness. ⁵ God called the light Day, and the darkness he called Night. And there was evening and there was morning, the first day.

Hebrews 11:3 ³ By faith we understand that the worlds were framed by the word of God, <u>so that the things which are seen were not made of things which are visible.</u>

I believe this also points toward a holographic simulation.

The Ultimate Simulation

Mystery within the mystery.

Genesis chapter one is a prophetic description of the making of the Sons of God. It is an allegory of the process by which sons are made into His image. It is also the template by which God creates.

Romans 8:19 [19] For the earnest expectation of the creation eagerly <u>waits for the revealing of the sons of God</u>.

Day 1

Nothing happens in this process of creating sons until Jesus, the light of the world, enters into our heart. We are empty and void until He appears in our heart.

Day 2

Genesis 1:6-8 [6] And God said, "Let there be an expanse in the midst of the waters, and let it separate the waters from the waters." [7] And God made the expanse and <u>separated the waters that were under the expanse from the waters that were above the expanse. And it was so.</u> [8] And <u>God called the expanse Heaven.</u> And there was evening and there was morning, the second day.

Where is the kingdom of heaven?

Luke 17:20-21 [20] Now when He was asked by the Pharisees when the kingdom of God would come, He answered them and said, "The kingdom of God does not come with observation; [21] nor will they say, 'See here!' or 'See there!' <u>For indeed, the kingdom of God is within you."</u>

The Ultimate Simulation

The next step is the separating of the soul and spirit by the Word of God. The waters above are separated from the waters below.

Hebrews 4:12 [12] For the word of God *is* living and powerful, and sharper than any two-edged sword, piercing even to the division of soul and spirit, and of joints and marrow, and is a discerner of the thoughts and intents of the heart.

Day 3

Genesis 1:9-13 [9] And God said, "Let the waters under the heavens be gathered together into one place, and let the dry land appear." And it was so. [10] God called the dry land Earth, and the waters that were gathered together he called Seas. And God saw that it was good.

[11] And God said, "Let the earth sprout vegetation, plants yielding seed, and fruit trees bearing fruit in which is their seed, each according to its kind, on the earth." And it was so. [12] The earth brought forth vegetation, plants yielding seed according to their own kinds, and trees bearing fruit in which is their seed, each according to its kind. And God saw that it was good. [13] And there was evening and there was morning, the third day.

Day three is the production of fertile soil in the heart for the planting, growing and producing fruit.

Ask the Lord to reveal days 4 and 5.

The Ultimate Simulation

It's interesting on the sixth day God did not <u>create</u> man, but <u>made</u> him in His image. Something that will happen when Jesus returns.

2 Peter 3:8 [8] But, beloved, do not forget this one thing, that <u>with the Lord one day is as a thousand years</u>, and a thousand years as one day.

Does each day in Genesis chapter one represent a thousand years in the making of a son process? In 2020 the current Hebrew year is 5780, which means there are only 220 years until the beginning of the seventh day as prophesied in Genesis 1. We are in day 6 when we are to be made into the image of God.

1 John 3:2 [2] Beloved, now we are children of God; and it has not yet been revealed what we shall be, but <u>we know that when He is revealed, we shall be like Him</u>, for we shall see Him as He is.

Jesus is coming soon. How soon?

Here are a couple of scriptures that I believe have clues.

Joshua 3:1-4 [1] Then Joshua rose early in the morning; and they set out from Acacia Grove and came to the Jordan, he and all the children of Israel, and lodged there before they crossed over. [2] So it was, after three days, that the officers went through the camp; [3] and they commanded the people, saying, "When you see the ark of the covenant of the LORD your God, and the priests, the Levites, bearing it, then you shall set out from your place and go after it. [4] <u>Yet there shall be a space between you and it, about two</u>

The Ultimate Simulation

thousand cubits by measure. Do not come near it, that you may know the way by which you must go, for you have not passed *this* way before."

The Lord told me ***"This scripture is also prophetic and cubits are years."***

Notice it says "about". It has been almost 2000 years since the Ark (Jesus) entered the Promised Land. Joshua chapter 4 says the priests carrying the ark stood in the dry river bed while the people crossed. Basically, the priests and ark represent an intercession allowing an uncrossable expanse to be crossable. After the people crossed 12 stones from the river were put where the priests were standing and 12 stones were put at the new camp. Upon completion the priests carried the ark out of the river bed. As soon as their feet touched regular land, the water started to flow again.

Hebrews 7:25 [25] Therefore He is also able to save to the uttermost those who come to God through Him, since He always lives to make intercession for them.

Just like the priest with the ark, Jesus intercedes for us to allow us to cross over to the promised land. Does this mean that at sometime this access by grace will end?

Matthew 24:21-22 [21] For then there will be great tribulation, such as has not been since the beginning of the world until this time, no, nor ever shall be. [22] And unless those days were shortened, no flesh would be saved; but for the elect's sake those days will be shortened.

Do the math and realize it is sooner.

The Ultimate Simulation

Genesis 6:3 ³ And the LORD said, "My Spirit shall not strive with man forever, for he *is* indeed flesh; yet his days shall be one hundred and twenty years."

The Hebrew word above for years, sheneh, could be translated as lifetimes or generations. By my calculations we are approximately 120 generations since Adam.

Some believe the Genesis 6:3 scripture relates to the time on the earth for the Holy Spirit. Considering the Azuza Street revival began on April 14, 1906 with an outpouring of the Holy Spirit. Add 120 years and you see where I'm going. Maybe both are correct.

Possibilities.

Chapter 14: Forces and Particles

I believe there are seven forces in the universe because there are seven spirits before the throne of God. As a programmer, in binary the value of the first three bits are 1, 2 and 4 which add up to 7. There are seven combinations of these three. Each force related to a specific combination. As of today, there are four and possibly 5 forces. They are gravity, electromagnetism, greater nuclear and lesser nuclear forces. X17 is a possible new force. Based upon binary 1,2,4, I think the Father has one, the Holy Spirit has two and the Son has three. Since the Son is about matter, the greater nuclear, lesser nuclear and X17 forces are His. The Father is one so I attribute gravity to Him. That leaves two for the Holy Spirit who draws people to God. Electromagnetism is the only known one left. Then there needs to be a second. I concluded there needed to be a force I call micromagnetism that controls the orientation of fields that make up the holographic time/space matrix. I don't have a Word on this, but it sounds good and will serve as a place keeper until further revelation.

Revelation 4:5 ⁵ From the throne came flashes of lightning, and rumblings and peals of thunder, <u>and before the throne were burning seven torches of fire, which are the seven spirits of God,</u>

Why are there seven?

The Ultimate Simulation

There is one for each combination of the trinity.

1. Father
2. Holy Spirit
3. Son
4. Father & Son
5. Father & Holy Spirit
6. Son & Holy Spirit
7. Father, Son & Holy Spirit

In the natural, these would be:

1. Gravity — Father
2. Magnetism — Holy Spirit
3. Micromagnetism (my term) — Father & Holy Spirit
4. Strong nuclear force — Son
5. Weak nuclear force — Son & Father
6. X17 — Son & Holy Spirit
7. Supernatural power — Father, Holy Spirit & Son

(Accessed by faith through unity with what God has said).

The first six forces are subject to the seventh.

There is a lot more here. I am still working on it.

The Ultimate Simulation

24 Particles

Since I believe the descriptions of heaven are also descriptions of creation, it may be that the 24 elders are 24 particles. Each made up of combinations of the primary field and its three states.

Revelation 4:4 [4] Around the throne *were* twenty-four thrones, and on the thrones I saw twenty-four elders sitting, clothed in white robes; and they had crowns of gold on their heads.

Since the number of man is 6, it's a possibility this dimension is based upon Lie Group E6 yielding 24 particles. The next dimension could be based upon Lie Group E7 yielding 52 particles and the upper dimension based upon Lie Group E8 yielding 120 particles.

My figuring is probably wrong, but I'm trying to get a glimpse of the possibilities of what the upper dimensions are like with all the other particles.

It occurs to me that Lie Group E8 would be the perfect model for a simulation of this size for optimum smoothness.

I'm not a mathematician; I just read a lot and wonder.

Chapter 15: Eternal Life and God's Love

In a simulation, eternity is for as long as the simulation runs or as long as the sub-simulation is in effect. It could also mean life beyond or outside the simulation. It is not hard to imagine that the maker of so complex a simulation would have the ability to transfer an AI to an outside vehicle. Another possibility may be the merger with the control AI.

God's Love

I believe God's love is available to all. However, I cannot find a scripture that says it is unconditionally ours. God's love extends to those who embrace Him, His laws, precepts, statutes, judgments and commandments. It is appropriated by our acceptance of Him and His word.

John 14:21 [21] He who has My commandments and keeps them, it is he who loves Me. <u>And he who loves Me will be loved by My Father</u>, and I will love him and manifest Myself to him.

1 John 4:15-16 [15] <u>Whoever confesses that Jesus is the Son of God, God abides in him, and he in God.</u> [16] And we have known and believed the love that God has for us. God is love, and he who abides in love abides in God, and God in him.

The above scriptures are conditional.

I addressed this earlier. I believe God loves what we can become. His love extends to us, but it is of no use

The Ultimate Simulation

to us unless we appropriate it by faith and an ever deepening relationship of obedience and discovery of Him.

Chapter 16: Were We Seeded?

Not in the sense you think. I believe God lets the simulation play out. When an architected life form develops to where there is potential for sonship, then God steps in and breaths into them the breath of life, which includes free will, a measure of faith, the authority to have dominion and a hole or desire that can only be filled by Him. How He does this is not in scripture. If we're in a simulation, then one of His agents is tasked with the job. It maybe that there is a race of aliens (watchers) whose sole purpose is to look for emerging life and help them along into the direction of sonship. It may also be there is another race of aliens (tormentors) under the direction of a fallen angel whose job is to collect souls for torment. It maybe those souls that are cast into outer darkness try to take possession of bodies for what they think is a second chance (demons). It may be ...

If we are in a simulation then these sonship attributes must have a physical reality. Whether it's DNA, RNA, blood, some yet to be discovered mechanism or all of the above, it has to exist. We do know that stress changes DNA. I also believe there are physical ramifications to spiritual improvement/decline. When our name gets added to the Lamb's book of life, we are now eligible to receive the down payment via the Holy Spirit that opens up new possibilities. The limitations that apply to human beings are now exchanged with those associated with sonship. To the extent we activate them by faith determines their manifestation and our transformation. Being born again is

The Ultimate Simulation

really about new possibilities. The more we cling to humanity, the more we deny the gift of God.

John 6:53-56 ⁵³ So Jesus said to them, "Truly, truly, I say to you, <u>unless you eat the flesh of the Son of Man and drink his blood, you have no life in you.</u> ⁵⁴ Whoever feeds on my flesh and drinks my blood has eternal life, and I will raise him up on the last day. ⁵⁵ For my flesh is true food, and my blood is true drink. ⁵⁶ Whoever feeds on my flesh and drinks my blood abides in me, and I in him.

Years ago, the Lord said to me **"In order to succeed here, you must take the attitude of a resident alien".**

My humanity was crucified with Christ. The problem is my mind hasn't accepted it. My mind wants to go back to Egypt, where I didn't need to change and my basic needs were met. Religion tells you it's for after you go to heaven, but scripture says it's for now.

Luke 17:21 ²¹ nor will they say, 'See here!' or 'See there!' <u>For indeed, the kingdom of God is within you.</u>"

2 Corinthians 6:1-2 ¹ We then, *as* workers together *with Him* also plead with *you* not to receive the grace of God in vain. ² For He says: "In an acceptable time I have heard you, and in the day of salvation I have helped you." <u>Behold, now *is* the accepted time; behold, now *is* the day of salvation</u>.

I got a little off track.

Matthew 3:7-9 ⁷ But when he saw many of the Pharisees and Sadducees coming to his baptism, he said to

The Ultimate Simulation

them, "Brood of vipers! Who warned you to flee from the wrath to come? [8] Therefore bear fruits worthy of repentance, [9] and do not think to say to yourselves, 'We have Abraham as *our* father.' <u>For I say to you that God is able to raise up children to Abraham from these stones.</u>

    The above scripture points to the possibility of God seeding us. I believe the building blocks of DNA have been found in meteors. Were these rocks then seedings from God or one of His agents or was it just the simulation playing out? Was a specific DNA seeded to see how it would develop? Are those that show promise continued and those that do not destroyed?

    Since there are living creatures with four faces before the throne of God, it looks like they were intentionally seeded.

Chapter 17: What's Next?

If you can't figure it out from what is put forward here, telling you won't mean anything. This is where you need an 'Aha' moment from the Holy Spirit. I have seen a glimpse of mine, but I have no idea what your possibilities are.

1 Corinthians 2:9-10 [9] But as it is written: "Eye has not seen, nor ear heard, nor have entered into the heart of man the things which God has prepared for those who love Him." [10] But God has revealed *them* to us through His Spirit. For the Spirit searches all things, yes, the deep things of God.

Jeremiah 29:11 [11] For I know the thoughts that I think toward you, says the LORD, thoughts of peace and not of evil, to give you a future and a hope.

Proverbs 25:2 [2] *It is* the glory of God to conceal a matter, but the glory of kings *is* to search out a matter.

Ephesians 3:20-21 [20] Now to Him who is able to do exceedingly abundantly above all that we ask or think, according to the power that works in us, [21] to Him *be* glory in the church by Christ Jesus to all generations, forever and ever. Amen.

Unless your relationship with God is more than a child, receiving this revelation is probably not going to happen.

The Ultimate Simulation

John 16:12 [12] "I still have many things to say to you, but you cannot bear *them* now.

Revelation 21 describes a large cube craft descending from heaven almost 1400 miles per side.

Revelation 21:10-21 [10] And he carried me away in the Spirit to a great and high mountain, and showed me the great city, the holy Jerusalem, descending out of heaven from God, [11] having the glory of God. Her light *was* like a most precious stone, like a jasper stone, clear as crystal. [12] Also she had a great and high wall with twelve gates, and twelve angels at the gates, and names written on them, which are *the names* of the twelve tribes of the children of Israel: [13] three gates on the east, three gates on the north, three gates on the south, and three gates on the west.

[14] Now the wall of the city had twelve foundations, and on them were the names of the twelve apostles of the Lamb. [15] And he who talked with me had a gold reed to measure the city, its gates, and its wall. [16] The city is laid out as a square; its length is as great as its breadth. And he measured the city with the reed: twelve thousand furlongs. Its length, breadth, and height are equal. [17] Then he measured its wall: one hundred *and* forty-four cubits, *according* to the measure of a man, that is, of an angel. [18] The construction of its wall was *of* jasper; and the city *was* pure gold, like clear glass. [19] The foundations of the wall of the city *were* adorned with all kinds of precious stones: the first foundation *was* jasper, the second sapphire, the third chalcedony, the fourth emerald, [20] the fifth sardonyx, the sixth sardius, the seventh chrysolite, the eighth beryl, the ninth topaz, the tenth chrysoprase, the eleventh jacinth, and the twelfth amethyst. [21] The twelve gates *were* twelve pearls: each individual gate was of one

The Ultimate Simulation

pearl. <u>And the street of the city *was* pure gold, like transparent glass.</u>

What host of heaven built it, what powers it and does it have a crew? What is transparent gold? It sounds like a giant Borg cube. In a simulation, all these questions have answers. In the end, will we be assimilated?

Secondary logical possibilities

I don't have scripture for these yet. However, I did want to capture them as this is a work in progress.

No.	Description
1	There is a high probability that this simulation was written by AI.
2	Due to its complexity and completeness, this is not version 1.
3	There are billions of other farms.
4	The singularity at the core of the black hole acts as an aperture.
5	Reality bubbles are not static, but either expanding or contracting. This would change the red shift painted onto the reality bubble to make it seem that objects outside the black hole were accelerating/ decelerating faster than predicted.
6	If the bubble were collapsing, we wouldn't see it coming. Although it could be inferred.

The Ultimate Simulation

7	If an object was captured by this black hole with a singularity, would it have memory after squeezing through the singularity?
8	What else could the 24 elders be representative of?
9	Can reality bubbles intersect?
10	Why is there a green crystal structure around the throne? Could it be a source of power?
11	Is a white hole the back end of a ruptured black hole?
12	Could we be living in a black hole which is itself inside a black hole?
13	Since there appear to be repeating patterns, could each of the three main overlays be fractals with variations of the Golden Rule?
14	Since it appears everything is based off of 3, could pi be the basis for the Holy Spirit layer as it is 3 with uncertainty?

Conclusions

I would that you would think, decide and act. In the end, simulation or not, it is the Word of God which is true and the outcome is the same. If this is a simulation, then hundreds of prophecies in the Bible written over a thousand years all being fulfilled in Jesus would not be out of the ordinary. If this is a simulation, God exists and His word is absolutely true. It would also be the most marvelous piece of engineering we will ever experience. Whether this simulation is playing in a computer or the mind of God or in the mind of God in a computer, don't you want to see how deep the rabbit hole goes?

The Bible is the most incredible document ever written. There are mysteries within mysteries, but in depth revelation only comes through the Holy Spirit. Everything is there. If we are living in a simulation, it doesn't change the Word of God one iota. It does, however, change your perspective.

Truth is a point. We all observe it from different perspectives. Perspectives are real, but are not the truth. The only way we can grow in the knowledge of the truth is to periodically change our perspective and resolve any anomalies.

The Ultimate Simulation

> **Conclusion: I believe we are living in a holographic simulation in a reality bubble inside a black hole. I believe our future is to explore, develop possibilities and create opportunities for more sons of God to develop. I believe within each person who receives Jesus are possibilities only they can fulfill through the Holy Spirit. One of our jobs as sons is to help others realize their potential in Christ.**

To me, my conclusions are real. Whether or not they are true, hopefully time will tell. Maybe in some other reality they are true. As long as I keep changing my perspective, my conclusions and reality will change and I will get closer to the truth. If there are parts of God's Word that don't work for you, maybe you need a perspective change. Quit trying to justify why it doesn't work and realize you're the problem. None of our possibilities can come to fruition until we repent, forgive and accept Jesus as Lord.

The rest of the vision.

(See the cover.)

I was suspended in a pea green void. Heaven and earth had disappeared without a sound. I looked in every direction and there was nothing except the bright light. How long I was there I don't know. Five minutes or five millennia, there was no way to tell. I don't recall seeing I

The Ultimate Simulation

had a body. After a long silence, a voice came. "**Say it**". What was I supposed to say? I thought about it and was still confused about the meaning. The voice came again, **"Say it"**. In an instant I knew what was required. I said "Let there be Light". And the place exploded in light.

I am not Jesus. I am not God. I am a redeemed, flawed and in-training potential son of the most-high God. I explore possibilities for the manifestation and development of future offspring and anything else the Holy Spirit says. In Christ, all things that He says are possible are possible.

If you want to have a future with your possibilities, then say this prayer:

Jesus, come into my heart. I believe You are the Son of God. I confess my sin and want to be a part of Your kingdom now and in the future. Help me to explore Your possibilities for me.

Father, open up my eyes, my ears, my heart and my mind to your Word and the Holy Spirit, that it may be meat to my bones and life to my soul, always lifting the name of Jesus with joy, so Your Kingdom may be extended in me and through me. **All to Your glory**.

The Ultimate Simulation

      I just purchased theultimatesimulation.com and am setting up a website to continue to develop this book. Any comments or suggestions should be directed to it. Hopefully it will be operational by the time you read this.

An Urgent Prayer

O Father, great and fearsome God. You never waver in your covenant commitment, never give up on those who love you, love your Son, Jesus, and do what you say.

Yet, we have sinned, committed iniquity, rebelled, and loved less than required, even by departing from your precepts, your judgments, your Word and even your Presence. We have worshipped other gods of money, self, nationality, race, sexuality and political correctness, just to name a few.

We've turned a deaf ear to your Holy Spirit, your Word and your servants the prophets, who preach your Word to our leaders, our forefathers, and all the people in the land. We have robbed you in tithes and offerings and we have not given the land a Sabbath day's rest.

You have done everything right, Father, but all we have to show for our lives is guilt and shame, the whole lot of us—people of

(Add your city, State, Country)

at home and abroad.

The Ultimate Simulation

Oh yes, Father, we've been exposed in our shame, all of us—our leaders, judges, parents and forefathers — before the whole world. And deservedly so, because of our sin, rebellion, twistedness and complacency.

Your mercy and grace are our only hope, Father, since in our rebellion we've forfeited our rights.

We paid no attention to you when you told us how to live, the clear teaching that comes through your Word and the leading of the Holy Spirit.

All of us here ignore what you say. We defy your instructions and do what we please. And now we're paying for it: The solemn curses written out plainly in the revelation to God's servant Moses are now doing there work among us, the wages of our sin against you.

You are doing to us and our leaders what you said you would do: You are bringing catastrophic disaster on us!

Just as written in God's revelation to Moses, the catastrophe was total. Nothing was held back. We've kept at our sinning, never giving you a second thought, oblivious to your clear warning, and so you have no choice but to let the disaster loose on us in full force.

We think we're good, but don't know we are wretched, miserable and poor.

You, our Father, have a perfect right to do this since we persistently and defiantly ignore you.

The Ultimate Simulation

Father, you are our God, for you delivered your people from the land of Egypt in a show of power, in your name America was founded and prospered until now. We confess that we have sinned, that we have behaved wickedly, turning our back on you and even denying you. We justify killing babies and every sexual perversion just like Baal and Ashtoreth worshipers. We call sin not sin and righteousness we ridicule.

Our leaders are like the Pharisees heaping burdens upon the people while they drink and laugh. They make lofty speeches and say they know you, but they are like open tombs.

Following the precedents of what you have always done in setting things right, setting people right, please stop being so angry with America and your Church. We know it's our fault that this has happened, all because of our sins, iniquities and rebellions and our parents' likewise, and now we're an embarrassment to everyone around us. We know that judgment begins in the house of the Lord. We humble ourselves before you and accept your righteous punishment.

Father, hear this determined prayer of your servants. Have mercy on your weak and errant Church. Act out of who you are, not out of what we are.

Turn your ears our way, Father, and listen. Open your eyes and take a long look at this place and your servants. Open our ears so that we may hear again. We

The Ultimate Simulation

know that we don't deserve a hearing from you. Our appeal is to your mercy and grace. You are our only hope:

Father, listen to us! Father, forgive us!

Purge us with hyssop, and we shall be clean: wash us, and we shall be whiter than snow. Make us to hear joy and gladness; that the bones which thou hast broken may rejoice. Hide thy face from our sins, and blot out all our iniquities.

Create in us a clean heart, O God; and renew a right spirit within us. Cast us not away from thy presence; and take not thy Holy Spirit from us. Restore unto us the joy of thy salvation; and uphold us with thy free spirit. Then will we teach transgressors thy ways; and sinners shall be converted unto thee. (Psalms 51:7-13)

Father, look at us through the blood of Jesus, bring us back to our first love and fulfill your glorious promises!

(Add your promises from God here).

We believe you said that through unity of your church, you would bring revival to our children; you would display your glory in us. You promised me I would see Isa.60. "Arise, shine; for thy light has come, and the glory of the Lord is risen upon thee." Not only I, but all those whose hearts and hands are clean. Then there would be

The Ultimate Simulation

other miraculous signs and wonders drawing people to Christ...

Father, don't delay! Fulfill your promises.

Your Church and your people named after you need you more than ever: Jesus gave his life for us!

Adapted from Daniel 9:3-19 according to the prescription for iniquity, rebellion and sin in Leviticus 26:40-41.

T.Long - 6/1/2015

Other Books by Tom Long

Now that you've completed a Christian walk, what's next? According to Psalm 23, the Lord is with us when we walk. *"Yea, though I <u>walk</u> through the valley of the shadow of death, I will fear no evil: <u>for thou art with me;</u> thy rod and thy staff they comfort me"* (KJV). Where is He when it's time to stand?

ISBN 978-0-9718631-1-8   Paperback   200 pages

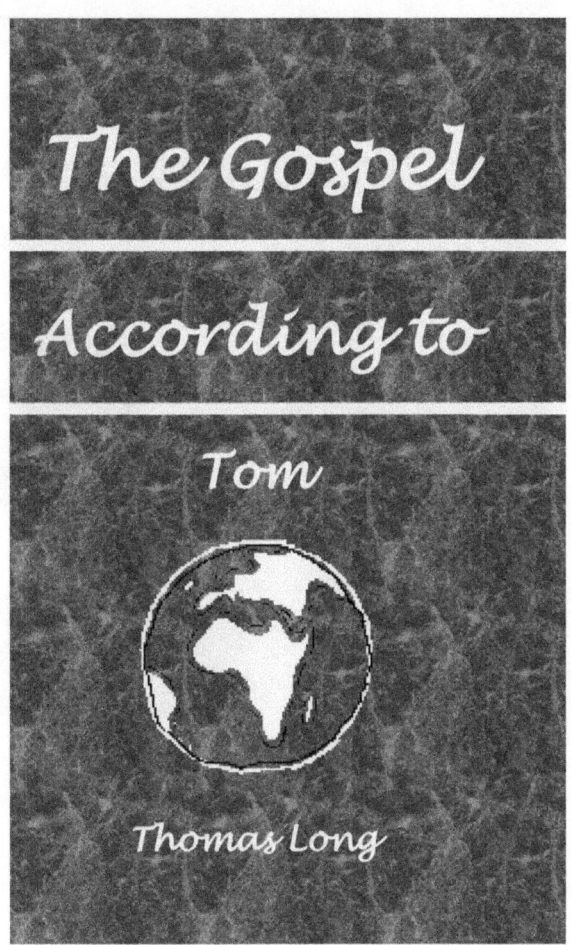

The meaning of the word *gospel* is "good news." To me, if the Gospel isn't good news, then I don't want it. If the Good News comes at a price, it's still good news as opposed to something that isn't available to me. Good News brings hope. Good News lifts me into the realm of possibilities. Good News expands my limits and introduces options I didn't have before. Good News isn't always happy or to my liking. It can be like "the worst terrorist in the world driving off a cliff in my new car." Good News is news that is in my best interest. In a nutshell, our view of the Gospel of Jesus Christ is like the love of a parent for a child from the child's point of view. This is my point of view. – *Tom Long*

ISBN 978-0-9718631-0-1   Paperback   174 pages

The Link

By Tom Long

The gap between God and man is the substance of religion. According to Michelangelo's famous fresco, God has made the first move by lifting His finger. This book is about the process of completing the link. Jesus said, *"But as many as received him, to them gave he power to become the sons of God, even to them that believe on his name"* (John 1:12).

ISBN 978-0-9718631-3-2   Paperback   126 pages

www.ingramcontent.com/pod-product-compliance
Lightning Source LLC
LaVergne TN
LVHW011912080426
835508LV00007BA/503